PORTRAITS OF GOD'S PEOPLE

Radiant Study Series

Edited by

MELISSA MCFERRIN

and

AUTUMN RICHARDSON

CYPRESS

Copyright © 2024 by Autumn Richardson

Manufactured in the United States of America

Cataloging-in-Publication Data

Portraits of God's people. Radiant study series/ edited by Autumn Richardson and Melissa McFerrin.

p. cm.

ISBN 978-1-956811-69-8 (pbk.) 978-1-956811-70-4 (ebook)

1. Bible—Study and teaching. I. Richardson, Autumn, editor. II. McFerrin, Melissa, editor. III. Title. IV. Series.

220.07—dc20

Library of Congress Control Number: 2024942912

For information:

Cypress Publications
3625 Helton Drive
PO Box HCU
Florence, AL 35630

www.hcu.edu

Contents

How to Use This Book

THANK you for picking up (or downloading) a copy of *Portraits of God's People*. This book is part of the Radiant Study Series and is a labor of love created by a team of women passionate about providing resources to enrich your Bible study, whether that happens on your own or with a group. That's why you'll see several extras at the end of each chapter and in the back of the book. Feel free to use as much or as little of the supplemental material as fits your situation.

As a result of feedback received from a survey of the Radiant Facebook group, this book is eight chapters, as opposed to the common thirteen-week study often formatted for a Bible class quarter. The great thing about the book, however, is that it is flexible. You can do an eight-week study, stretch it to thirteen weeks, or take it at whatever pace suits you or your group. Here is a suggested schedule for those who need the thirteen-week format to fit their congregation's Bible class schedule:

Portraits of God's People is a book about the church—who we are to God, who God is to us, and who we are to each other. Because the church is so unique, so special, and so diverse, God uses word pictures to help us understand. (For all you English grammarians out there: Yes, I know there are analogies, similes, allusions, and metaphors, but for the sake of simplicity, we're going to stick with the word "metaphor" throughout the book. Please forgive us.)

These portraits are special glimpses into the imagination and genius of God. He uses the ordinary to help us understand the extraordinary, elaborating on and emphasizing important aspects of life in the church with these metaphors. They vary in how often they are mentioned and in how far you can take the comparisons. We've chosen eight that appear as extended metaphors throughout the narrative of Scripture. In Appendix D, you will find a list of other comparative language God uses for the church. We encourage you to study those portraits on your own when you complete the chapters in the book.

At the end of each chapter, you'll find a prayer meant to direct your thoughts to God from the standpoint of the metaphor you've just studied. You can see the prayers all together in Appendix A.

After the prayer, you'll find three sets of questions:

1. Foundational Questions
2. Group Discussion
3. Personal Reflection

The Foundational Questions are the same for each chapter. They are key thoughts to consider for any word picture God uses for the church. If you decide to study the additional list in Appendix D, you'll want to use these questions for that as well.

Group Discussion questions will guide the interactive part of a study if you are using the book in a class or small group. These questions are geared toward how we can collectively live out these metaphors in God-honoring ways in our churches.

The Personal Reflection section is exactly what it sounds like. These questions will ask you to dig deeply into your attitudes, past experiences, and future intentions. For that reason, they may be most suitable for journaling on your own or discussing with a close friend. All of the questions have been collected in Appendix B, and permission is granted for you to make copies of Appendix B for private or church use. If you are studying this book in a class, those pages would make great handouts as take-home activities.

Appendix C contains a month's worth of additional Scriptures to go along with each chapter. We would encourage you to use them for Scripture copying or Bible marking, but they can simply serve for further reading and study as well. You may make copies of Appendix C too. If you plan to send home the Personal Reflection questions, consider adding these Scriptures to the sheet, and your class will be equipped to meditate on this material long after the class has ended.

Finally, there is a short conclusion as the book wraps up. You'll find some final thoughts and a set of questions designed to guide you in thinking back on the use of metaphors as a whole.

There are so many possibilities for how to use this book. Now it's your turn. Dive in and learn more about who you are to God, who He is to His people, and who we are supposed to be to each other!

Introduction

Ava Johnson

CONNECTION: We crave it. We seek it. We flourish with it. Connection grounds us and makes us feel safe. Although we can survive alone, we thrive when we work together. God designed His people to be communal creatures, and He desires His church to have the characteristics outlined in this book, *A Portraits of God's People.*

I am blessed to have a wonderful Christian family, and I pray that I can continue the legacy that my parents and grandparents have set. I want to be everything for my children; I want to exhibit every fruit of the Spirit flawlessly. I want to be a servant, a leader, a homemaker, a professional, a soft place to land, a giver of tough love, a gourmet chef, a costume designer, a number one fan, the Proverbs 31 woman, the Titus 2 woman, a friend, a parent—and to know exactly when to put on the exact hat that the child in front of me needs at that moment and then be ready for the next child with his individual needs with that hat in hand. I hope to be everything for my kids, but I am so very aware of all my shortcomings and human limitations.

I love the church, too. Without the church, my kids would be limited in their exposure to wonderful people with more wisdom than I could ever dream of. They would be subjected to me juggling all the hats that I think I should be wearing and getting it wrong most of the time. I always misunderstood the prominent phrase, "It takes a village." I always took it to mean that children are such handfuls that it takes hundreds of people to take turns wrestling them into submission. Now that I am a mom, there is still some wrestling, but I understand that it takes influence from my village to make well-rounded, productive adults out of my children. There is no better village than God's people!

I would like to think I am an adventurous person, but lately, it has been obvious how much I enjoy being home. Recently, I had a hard time staying away for a mere 48 hours for a retreat 20 minutes from my house. The lodging was beautiful, right on the lake, with a pool, hot tub, and nugget ice machine. The company was fantastic, women who love God and want to be a part of an amazing program to help women grow closer to God. The weather was perfect. There was nothing to complain about except I wanted to be home. I could not wrap my mind around it since my family and I had traveled earlier that year to Georgia and Texas, and I did not miss my house one time, but now I wanted to be in my messy house with my messy family rocking my messy bun. All of the ladies there were very gracious and patient with me as I tried to relax and focus on the retreat. When the retreat was over and I finally went home, I felt so much relief as soon as I stepped in my door. The sense of familiarity filled my soul. I realized as soon as I laid eyes on my kids and husband that they are the reason I am a homebody, not my messy house. They are my home, my comfort, my people.

That is how God wants us to feel in the church. He wants us to feel like this is where we are supposed to be. He wants us to be able to rest easy, knowing there is space for us. He wants us to feel a sense of relief as soon as we walk through the door, overwhelmed with the familiar feeling of love. He wants us to be connected.

I want to be around people who are of one mind in Christ but have unique strengths, qualities, talents, and opinions. The world tells us that we cannot get along with people who have different personalities, different views, or different skin colors. In a world that focuses on differences, God's people know that our differences are what make us the church. The church is strong, not because we are all mindless robots that exclude people who are different, but because we are all unique pieces that come together in an attempt to reflect God's light into a dark world. Our God does a beautiful job of portraying this idea of differences coming together in the metaphors He uses throughout His word. He wants us to be together. He wants us to build relationships. He wants us to be connected.

> *A blank canvas is where we all start—*
> *Endless possibilities to create art.*
>
> *When you hear "a portraits of God's people,"*
> *Do you think pews, preachers, and a steeple?*
> *Shiny, happy people with a smile on each face,*
> *The little children of the world in every race,*
> *Their Sunday best pressed without wrinkle or*
>   *stain,*
> *Who present themselves well without any strain?*
>
> *Or does your vision resemble your own life?*

A struggling mom, a lonely wife?
A young lady with no direction,
No sight of a purpose, no sense of connection?
Are you unsatisfied with the portrait He has
    designed,
Wondering why this was the one you were
    assigned?

Other portraits seem tidy and neat—
Clean lines, confident strokes, complete.

Why would He make ours such a mess?
Colored with trauma, worry, anxiety, and stress,
Out of focus, on a grayscale,
No signs of vibrancy or even pastel.

When we look closely at others' portraits, we
    can see
The beauty hidden between colors where you
    wouldn't think it would be.

The reason we do not always see the flaws of
    others,
Sometimes unheard of, that may cause you to
    shudder,
Is that the Painter turned "mistakes" into art
To hang in His gallery, to make them a part.
This gallery is filled with portraits of all—
Spiritual giants, humble servants, who heard the
    call.

God has a special place for you;
Still painting your portrait, He is not through.

He has navigated a path where you can be
    confident,
Surrounded by people your talents will
    complement.

Nestle into the place He placed you with pride
In the building, branch, body, as the bride.
Flock to the family in reverence to the priesthood
As a worker in the kingdom of a King who is good.

1

The Bride

Lori Boyd

IN 1549, Thomas Cranmer, the Archbishop of Canterbury, edited and published a collection of prayers and recitations for the Church of England entitled *The Book of Common Prayer*. The book, still in use today, contains the earliest recorded version of the standard wedding vows, which have not changed significantly over the years: "I, [name], take thee, [name], to my wedded (husband/wife), to have and to hold from this day forward, for better for worse, for richer for poorer, in sickness and in health, to love and to cherish, till death us do part, according to God's holy ordinance."[1] However, the book of Genesis, written thousands of years earlier, provides a powerful image of the marriage vow with these words: "Therefore a man shall leave his father and his mother and hold fast to his wife, and they shall become one flesh" (Gen 2:24 ESV). This was spoken in reference to the commitment between Adam and Eve, but on a deeper level, it was a prophecy about the coming Messiah—a Messiah who would leave His Father in heaven and come to the world to serve as the Husband of His beloved one. The relationship of Jesus to His church is symbolized in the Bible through His role as the Bridegroom, the church as His bride, the sacrificial and sanctifying love He demonstrated for her, and His fulfillment of the marriage vow that was first established in the garden of Eden.

ONE MAIN THING

Beginning in the Old Testament, extending through the Gospels, and even to the end of the New Testament, descriptions of God's relationship with His people use the image of a holy marriage, loving bridegroom, and chosen bride. In marriage, a bond is created between two people—a bond that is sealed with the promise of commitment. Since the beginning of time, this is the relationship God has sought with mankind. It is based on the premise of monogamy: He belongs to His people, and His people belong to Him.[2] In the Bible, the marriage commitment is often described in terms of a covenant. The Old Testament reveals that God established a covenant relationship with the Israelites. The covenant was made at Mt. Sinai with the Ten Commandments, in a sense, representing the marital vows.[3] The first commandment, "You shall have no other gods before me" (Exod 20:3), reflected God's expectation for Israel's level of commitment. No other god could be a husband to His people.

In Exodus 19:5–6, God told the Israelites that, if they obeyed His voice and kept His covenant, they would be His "treasured possession ... a kingdom of priests and a holy nation." However, time and again, Israel chose to be unfaithful, breaking the covenant with God and following after the gods of other nations. Their *idolatry* is often described in Scripture as *adultery*—the steepest violation one can make in a committed relationship.[4]

God filled the role of the Husband, and Israel, the perpetually unfaithful spouse.[5] God chose Israel to be His people above any other nation, not because of anything they had done to earn that position, but because of His love and mercy. He rescued them out of Egypt and gave them a home in the promised land. He delivered them time and again from enemies and various trials they faced. In return for His faithfulness, Israel was to recognize Him as the only God and keep His commandments. Despite this covenant relationship, Israel betrayed Him. In Jeremiah 3:20, God said through His prophet, "Surely, as a treacherous wife leaves her husband, so have you been treacherous to me, O house of Israel." Regardless of Israel's unfaithfulness, God continually forgave her and took her back when she cried out in desperation. This is illustrated in Psalm 106:44–45: "Nevertheless, He looked upon their distress, when He heard their cry. For their sake He remembered His covenant, and relented according to the abundance of His steadfast love." It is the covenant love of God that is key to understanding the divine side of the marriage relationship with Israel.[6] Throughout the time of the prophets, Israel was warned repeatedly about her unfaithfulness to God, but despite her sins, God promised a new covenant that would be made with all people: a covenant that would never be broken. In the book of Isaiah, the prophet foretells judgment on Israel for her disloyalty to God but also foretells her ultimate salvation. Isaiah 62:5, God said that He would rejoice over His people "as the bridegroom rejoices over the bride." There would be a new beginning for Israel, one that would find its perfect fulfillment in the new covenant sealed by the blood of the new Bridegroom, Jesus Christ.[7]

While God, in the Old Testament, is depicted as the Bridegroom, clearly this idea is shifted so that Jesus is represented as the Bridegroom in the New Testament.[8] In John 3:25–30, the disciples of John the Baptist questioned him about the people who were going to Jesus and being baptized. John reminded them that they had witnessed his testimony that he was not the Christ, but was sent before Him. Then he told them, "The one who has the bride is the bridegroom. The friend of the bridegroom, who stands and hears him, rejoices greatly at the bridegroom's voice. Therefore this joy of mine is now complete." This is the first time in the ministry of Jesus that He is referred to as the Bridegroom.

Jesus Himself made it known in Mark 2:19 when He said, "Can the wedding guests fast while the bridegroom is with them? As long as they have the bridegroom with them, they cannot fast." On the occasion of the wedding in Cana, described in John 2:1–11, Jesus's mother approached Him about the wine having run out. Jesus told the servants to fill up jars with water and then to take some out to give to the master of the feast. When the master tasted the water, it had turned into wine. Typically, at a wedding, it was the responsibility of the groom to supply the wine. The miracle that Jesus performed by turning water into wine demonstrated His role as the ultimate, long-awaited Bridegroom.

Also, in Paul's letter to the Corinthians, he warned them about false teachers and told them that he had betrothed them to one husband, referring to Christ (2 Cor 11:2). However, this was not a distinction only for the Christians in Corinth. The Bible teaches that the bride of Christ is symbolic of an even larger group of people—those who are members of His body, the church. Paul wrote to the church in Ephesus, "For the husband is the head of the wife, even as Christ is the head of the church, his body, and is himself its Savior" (Eph 5:23). As there is just one husband, so there is just one bride.[9]

GOING DEEPER

In Scripture, the analogy of Jesus as the Bridegroom and the church as His bride becomes even more meaningful when considering their relationship to one another. The church must be prepared for her Husband by being pure and properly dressed, and Jesus demonstrated His love for the church in His willingness to die for her and His promise to sanctify her. There is no greater example of the love that a husband should have for his wife. Paul described this relationship in Ephesians 5:22–33. One author observed, "The whole passage is one great simile."[10]

One of the most significant features of a wedding is the bridal gown. The bridegroom waits in anticipation at the end of the aisle for the bride to appear in her beautiful gown. How do Christians receive their spiritual clothing? The Bible presents a picture of Jesus adorning His bride, the church, with garments that have been cleansed from all blemishes by His own blood.[11] "Husbands, love your wives, as Christ loved the church and gave himself up for her, that he might sanctify her, having cleansed her by the washing of water with the word, so that he might present the church to himself in splendor, without spot or wrinkle or any such thing, that she might be holy and without blemish" (Eph 5:25–27). The cleansing that Jesus provides for His bride, the church, is obtained through baptism. Acts 22:16 describes baptism as a washing away of sins, and 1 John 1:9 states that it is the blood of Jesus that "cleanse[s] us from all unrighteousness." The bride of Christ has been properly dressed and is ready to be presented to her Bridegroom when she has been properly cleansed through the purifying waters of baptism.

When Paul told the Corinthians they had been betrothed to one husband in 2 Corinthians 11:2, he also told them they should be presented to Christ as a pure virgin. The Merriam-Webster Dictionary defines "pure" as "spotless, stainless."[12] In the same way, the pure white wedding dress of a bride is without spots or stains. The garment worn by the church is not a physical wedding dress; instead, it is the character of the individuals who comprise the church after their cleansing. It is purity of the heart or, as James the brother of Jesus wrote, "to keep oneself unstained from the world" (Jas 1:27). To say that the church has no "spot or wrinkle" emphasizes that the bride of Christ is without moral blemish, defilement, or deformity.[13]

Christ will come again one day to receive His pure bride. The apostle John described this event in Revelation 21:2: "And I saw the holy city, new Jerusalem, coming down out of heaven from God, prepared as a bride adorned for her husband." The "holy city" is spiritually referring to the church, as seen in Hebrews 12:22, which calls it "the city of the living God, the heavenly Jerusalem." The city coming down in glorious form is a picture of purity. One author observed, "She has been true to her Beloved and her dress speaks of her innocence, fidelity, and joy."[14] It is the bride's responsibility to be ready when He comes. In the meantime, she keeps herself spotless and stainless by walking in the light and allowing the blood of Christ to continually cleanse her (1 John 1:7).

In the context of Ephesians 5:22–23, the love a husband has for his wife and the submission she has to him is compared to Christ's love for the church and her submission to Him. James Coffman, in his commentary, states, "The measure of love that husbands are commanded to give their wives is that of Christ's love of the church—a love that would die for the beloved." He continues to say that her submission is more than rewarded and justified by that type of love.[15] Certainly, the wife is also to love her husband, but the emphasis in the

Ephesians 5 text is for the husband, as the head, to love his wife.[16] The love that husbands are expected to show their wives is *agape* love—a love that demonstrates selfless, caring concern. The Bible teaches that the greatest love ever shown is the laying down of one's life for another (John 15:13). This is the love that Christ demonstrated for the church (Rom 5:8), and we are to make that type of love our model.[17]

The love that Paul was describing in Ephesians 5:25 is not only the husband's willingness to physically die for his wife, but also a willingness to figuratively die to himself. This is explained in Jay Lockhart and David Roper's *Truth for Today* commentary in this way: "He should be dead to insisting on his own way."[18] Kerry Knight adds to this by saying, "This means his interests, will, and desires become secondary to hers."[19] This is an unselfish love, a love that seeks the best for others. The sacrifice Christ made for the church, His bride, saved her. Albert Barnes states, "A husband should feel that it should be one great object of his life to promote the salvation of his wife."[20] If a husband loves his wife the way Christ loves the church, then he will make this his objective daily. The text in Ephesians does not make this love optional. The verb form of "love" used in this context is the imperative, meaning it is a command. Husbands are commanded to love their wives just as Christ loved the church.

Not only did Jesus sacrifice Himself for His bride, but He also sanctified her. He set her apart as His unique bride. "In order to be sanctified, one must withdraw or separate from what is unclean—that is, the world—and be set apart for God's holy purpose."[21] Peter wrote about the sanctification of the church in 1 Peter 2:9, in words reminiscent of God's promise to the Israelites at Mount Sinai: "But you are a chosen race, a royal priesthood, a holy nation, a people for his own possession, that you may proclaim the excellencies of him who called you out of darkness into his marvelous light." In Ephesians 5:26, Paul said that it was Christ who sanctified the church—set her apart—"having cleansed her by the washing of water with the word." It was discussed earlier that the washing of the water represents baptism, but this verse also mentions a washing with the word. "Word" in the context may be talking about the gospel that was being preached and was instructing people to be baptized for cleansing.[22] John 17:17 describes the word as having sanctifying power. Therefore, the sanctification of the church came about when Christ cleansed it by baptism along with the word. Both the water and the word were involved.[23] This is how the church continues to be sanctified today.

WRAPPING IT UP

Jesus as the Bridegroom and the church as His bride was a concept that was prophesied at the beginning of time in the Garden of Eden. In Ephesians 5:31–32, Paul quoted an Old Testament verse and then revealed something remarkable that had been unknown up to that point: "Therefore a man shall leave his father and mother and hold fast to his wife, and the two shall become one flesh. This mystery is profound, and *I am saying that it refers to Christ and the church*" (emphasis added). What was hidden before but is now revealed is that Genesis 2:24, about husbands and wives, references Christ and the church. Jesus—designated in Romans 5:14 as the antitype of Adam, the type—*left His Father* and became a man. As He died on the cross, *He left His mother* in the care of His friend, John. "When Jesus was dead, the soldiers pierced His side, the very side from which woman was created in Eden, and blood and water flowed from the wound—the creation of the church."[24] Jesus came to save the world from sin, but He also came to create a bride for Himself, from His own body (Eph 1:22–23). Since the very beginning of creation, it has always been about Christ and the church, and it will remain that way for all of eternity.

The Bible describes the church in multiple ways, but perhaps the most beautiful description of all is the church as the bride of Christ. Throughout Scripture, Jesus is portrayed as a Bridegroom with a sacrificial and sanctifying love, and the church as His bride—properly dressed, pure, and prepared for her Husband. Furthermore, in His role as the Bridegroom, Jesus fulfills the marriage prophecy that was made in the garden of Eden: leaving His Father and mother, designating His bride, and becoming one with her. Each member of His church fills the role of His bride, and each member has the responsibility to remain pure and faithful until the Bridegroom returns. In Revelation 19:7, hear the shout of the multitudes in heaven at the end of time: "Let us rejoice and exult and give him the glory, for the marriage of the Lamb has come, and his Bride has made herself ready."

PRAYER

Beloved God, form me into the bride You desire me to be. Lead me to grow in purity, faithfulness, and unwavering devotion to You as I await the return of the Bridegroom. Help me to remain spotless and continually cleansed by the precious blood of Jesus.

FOUNDATIONAL QUESTIONS

1. How would people living during the time of the

Bible have understood this metaphor in their historical and cultural context(s)?

2. How does God's choice of this metaphor help you better understand the way He views His people?

3. How does this metaphor enhance your understanding of the relationship between Christ and the church? Of your personal relationship with Jesus?

4. What does this metaphor help you learn about your *individual* role and *personal* responsibility as part of Christ's church?

5. How can the church as a *community* better embody this metaphor?

6. How might this metaphor help you explain the church to non-believers?

7. Are there any challenges that arise from misusing, misapplying, or over-emphasizing this metaphor?

GROUP DISCUSSION

1. In the Prophets, we see God's reactions to the unfaithfulness of His people, both His hurt and His forgiveness. What lessons can we learn from His character about honesty, accountability, and forgiveness in our own lives?

2. What are some ways that Christians, as Christ's bride, might live in adultery?

3. How does understanding baptism as a cleansing and preparation for Christ influence our view of this act? In what practical ways can the church ensure we are "properly dressed" as a bride waiting for Jesus's return?

4. How can we encourage others to see themselves as the bride of Christ and live accordingly?
5. Thinking about the theme of forgiveness in God's relationship with Israel, how can we mirror this in our church and community?

PERSONAL REFLECTION

1. Think of a time you were unfaithful to Christ. How did you, or can you, restore that relationship? In what ways did you, or can you, experience forgiveness and renewed commitment?
2. What specific actions and decisions can help you strengthen your commitment and faithfulness to Christ, similar to the way a wife continually commits to her husband?
3. How can you practice selfless, sacrificial love in your everyday interactions, mirroring Christ's love for the church?

2

The Family

Jeanne Foust

"So then, as we have opportunity, let us do good to everyone, and especially to those who are of the household of faith" (Gal 6:10 ESV).

ONE MAIN THING

FOR ALMOST SEVENTY-FIVE YEARS, American television networks have provided audiences with an insider's look at "family life." The Bradys, Bunkers, Clampetts, Cleavers, Cunninghams, Ewings, Huxtables, Ingallses, Jeffersons, Ricardos, Tanners, Taylors, Waltons, and countless others have offered us glimpses into fictional homes and imagined scenarios. They have provided us with a lifetime of wild, funny, difficult, memorable, and perhaps misrepresented pictures of family life. A few of these families gave us squeaky-clean, idyllic homes with wholesome conversations around a large dining table, but most portrayed a less-than-perfect—and sometimes downright dysfunctional—American family, where life, personalities, and challenges did battle while viewers tuned in faithfully. In the end, almost all the episodes ended in eighteen to twenty-two minutes with problems solved, closure, and resolution achieved ... until the next time.

Before we criticize these fictional depictions of family life too harshly, remember that when we turn to the Bible, we find messy families at every turn. As we thumb through the Old Testament, we can take our pick of families NOT to emulate. From the very first family onward, we see deception, jealousy, sibling rivalry, broken hearts, favoritism, wayward children, marital difficulties, cheating, lying, murder, affairs, and everything else. To be honest, it's hard to find more than a family or two we might consider above reproach—and that's in *Scripture!*

Yet, "family" is one of the ways God chooses to help us understand His church and how it works. *We are God's family.* This depiction may feel lacking (and we're bound to experience disappointment at every turn) if our expectation of family is defined by what we see on Christmas cards and social media —those photoshopped images of Pinterest-perfect gatherings and once-in-a-lifetime adventures. And if our perceptions are colored by the television family, well, we might feel better about our own family, but what does the comparison say about God's people?

"Family" is actually the perfect portrait to relate the realities of church life, because family relationships are, in fact, messy and imperfect but also rewarding and wonderful. Family life means hard work, and the same is true for our church family life. Just as members of functional families offer forgiveness and grace to one another as they learn to work through their differences, so must we as the church. We may not tie up all the problems in twenty-two minutes or fewer, but the redemption story in our church families is beautiful and worth the hard work.

GOING DEEPER

Familial love is a type of unconditional love often shared among family members, whether biological, adoptive, extended, or chosen. Greek scholars called this love *storge*, distinguishing it from *agape*, *philia*, and *eros*. It is the kind of love parents have for their children; it is the bond family members enjoy because they belong to and identify with the family. The many benefits of family are also available in God's family, into which each of us has been adopted through Jesus Christ (Eph 1:5). Those benefits are largely spiritual but can be physical and emotional as well. Being disciples of Jesus, we become connected to one another with bonds made strong by the sacrificial love demonstrated on the cross. We become a spiritual family with and for each other.

But why does God use the metaphor of family to describe His people if the concept of family is so hard to get right? In short, we humans are messy and difficult, so any group (family or church) composed of people is going to be imperfect. But just as we see beauty in our own imperfect families, God wants us to see that same beauty and unity in our brothers and sisters in Christ.

So let's look closer at how God describes us, His people, in terms of family:

1. *We are His children.* What an amazing thought! He is our Father—the perfect Father—who knows us by name. Regardless of whether our earthly fathers reflected God to us or not, we share a heavenly Father who is good, forgiving, and loving. First John 3:1 says, "See what kind of love the Father

has given to us, that we should be called children of God; and so we are." We have been adopted into God's family, chosen by the Creator of the universe to be His.

This idea cannot be a passing thought. Let's camp out here a moment and think about its profundity. In one of the most quoted and known passages of Scripture, John 3:16, we are told that God sacrificed His only Son so that we, His adopted sons and daughters, could anticipate and enjoy eternal life. Heaven is ours because God placed a high value on you and me as His children. When I look at the person sitting next to me in worship, when I see him or her through the eyes of God and Jesus, the value of my Christian family is clear.

As a mom, I know how much I want what's best for my children. How much more does God, the perfect Father, want what is best for us? He proved it at the cross, and He affirms it through His providential care for us. Let's relish the thought that His love is unfathomable, and that love extends not just to me, but to everyone in our church families.

2. *We are a family of believers.* When we look in Scripture, we see that the Bible uses family language to identify our relationships within the body of Christ. Paul refers to "our sister Phoebe, a servant of the church at Cenchreae" in Romans 16:1, and Peter sent his first letter through Silvanus, "a faithful brother as I regard him" (1 Pet 5:12). Paul describes his relationship with Timothy "as a son with a father" in Philippians 2:22. These descriptions speak of close connection—like family—and there are advantages to those kinds of connections within the body.

According to Galatians 6:10, we should do good to everyone, but "especially to those who are of the household of faith." Just as our families are united over any number of things—geography, shared experience, even something as silly as sports allegiance—we are united to our Christian family because we share the most important thing: We believe. Acts 4:32 describes the first-century church as having "everything in common." They were unified and gave sacrificially so that none among them was in need. The implication is not that we should or will agree on every point of discussion, but that we have a common bond because of our faith in the Father, Son, Holy Spirit, the inspired word of God, and this spiritual family.

The real key in any healthy physical or spiritual family is love. Paul tells us to "Love one another with brotherly affection. Outdo one another in showing honor" (Rom 12:10). I love the idea of outdoing one another in love and honor. What would happen if we tried that approach instead of keeping a scorecard of times we have been wronged, hurt, or disappointed?

3. *We are members of God's household.* We belong! We have identity! We have people pulling for us and wanting what's best for us. In a world so broken and segmented, belonging has become a missing link for many, but in God's perfect plan, He offered us—and everyone—a place to be welcomed and accepted. Rather than being "strangers and aliens," He calls us "fellow citizens with the saints" and "members of the household of God" (Eph 2:19).

This is the "brotherly love" described as *philia*. The word of God tells us "how one ought to behave in the household of God, which is the church of the living God, a pillar and buttress of the truth" (1 Tim 3:15), and if you remember the church hymn *God's Family*, you know how this kind of love looks: "Sometimes we laugh together, sometimes we cry ... ."[1] Good, bad, and ugly, we share our lives with our spiritual family, and the bond becomes even tighter and closer.

In all the applications of family above, we will not be perfect family members. God may be the perfect Father, but we will not be His ideal children and will need repeated forgiveness, which God, of course, offers generously and graciously. We will mess up in our relationships within the "family of believers," and apologies, as they say, will be in order. Also, we will not always be as welcoming to or accepting of outsiders, and we will have to admit our faults and make things right. "I'm sorry" is one of the most difficult things to say and mean, but families are the perfect places to practice it. In fact, humility is a virtue we all need to live peaceably with each other. As Philippians 2:3–4 reminds us, "Do nothing from selfish ambition or conceit, but in humility count others more significant than yourselves. Let each of you look not only to his own interests, but also to the interests of others." That humility will see us through tense situations and difficult times.

These hard moments aren't always fun. In fact, they hardly ever are, but we learn to grow up together. And in the process, our spiritual family, the family of God, becomes stronger and more committed to each other because we've traveled and learned together. "Finally, brothers," writes Paul in 2 Corinthians 13:11, "rejoice. Aim for restoration, comfort one another, agree with one another, live in peace; and the God of love and peace will be with you." These are tall orders for us humans, but our calling as sons and daughters of the King of kings is a high one, and our place in His kingdom and our role in His church are important.

WRAPPING IT UP

Family life can be one of the greatest joys on earth, but there are also difficult parts to work through. Families share time, memories, growing pains, inside jokes, history, and so much more, and we see each other at our absolute best and at our unfortunate, but very real, worst. Through our shared experiences, we learn, if we're going to be successful as a family, to stick it out together, offering forgiveness and grace early and often. We love each other, protect each other, and look out for each other's best interests.

Is this the picture God had in mind when He described His people, His church, in familial terms? We are not all the same, and we don't always agree, but we stick it out together, lean into each other's strengths, and offer forgiveness and grace as much as we need to. Despite the messiness of living our spiritual lives together, there is beauty and redemption in that shared story of being God's family. Until heaven, community and support are available through the beautiful imagery of, and the real life with, our church family.

There's no place like home. In my personal family, I always wanted our home to be a "soft place to fall." When the world "out there" was difficult and unkind, when the day had been hard or long, I wanted the people under my roof to know they were always welcomed and loved regardless. I wanted them to know someone would listen and try to understand or at least pray that tomorrow would be kinder to them. As I've gotten older, I've started to see how critical it is for the church to become that "soft place to fall," a kind, loving spiritual haven, however imperfect, where family gathers to rally around each other. I have to believe that's what everyone in the world wants and needs—insulation from the harshness, a place to belong. That's what family is, and when we do it well, it is a beautiful portrait of God's people.

PRAYER

 Abba Father, allow me to feel Your presence as my loving Father. You have given me a place where I am welcomed and accepted, and I thank You for Your providential care. Open my eyes to the family I have around me, and show me how to support and love my brothers and sisters in Christ.

FOUNDATIONAL QUESTIONS

1. How would people living during the time of the Bible have understood this metaphor in their historical and cultural context(s)?
2. How does God's choice of this metaphor help you better understand the way He views His people?
3. How does this metaphor enhance your understanding of the relationship between Christ and the church? Of your personal relationship with Jesus?
4. What does this metaphor help you learn about your *individual* role and *personal* responsibility as part of Christ's church?
5. How can the church as a *community* better embody this metaphor?
6. How might this metaphor help you explain the church to non-believers?
7. Are there any challenges that arise from misusing, misapplying, or over-emphasizing this metaphor?

GROUP DISCUSSION

1. Reflect on families in Scripture that were dysfunctional. Discuss why and how God still used them, even in their "messiness." How can this translate to our imperfect congregations?
2. What are some practices, rituals, and customs that families observe to remain strong and connected that are also important for spiritual families?
3. Why might some people struggle with the concept of church as a family? How can we help them?
4. What can our church do to help integrate new members into our spiritual community so they feel like part of the family and see us as their "soft place to fall"?
5. How can we model being a family as a congregation to our local community?

PERSONAL REFLECTION

1. Thinking about your family of origin, identify any areas where you struggle with the family metaphor and explore ways you can work to overcome those challenges.
2. Think about your roles in your local church. In what ways can you be a more supportive and loving sister?
3. What effect should being a "child of God" have on the way you view yourself? How should it influence the way you interact with others?

3

The Body

J.J. Davenport

TOES ARE NOT A BIG DEAL. Think about it. Toes are little. They don't require a lot of care, and they are generally hidden in a shoe. Toes are not a big deal—until they are. I recently broke my little toe when I stubbed it at home. It hurt for weeks. I walked weird. I had to wear special shoes and was so worried that someone would accidentally hurt it worse. My two-year-old enjoyed telling everyone I hurt my toe that went "'wee wee wee' all the way home." It was embarrassing how this one little toe had such a huge impact on my life. Toes aren't a big deal—or are they?

> For just as the body is one and has many members, and all the members of the body, though many, are one body, so it is with Christ. For in one Spirit we were all baptized into one body—Jews or Greeks, slaves or free—and all were made to drink of one Spirit. For the body does not consist of one member but of many. If the foot should say, "Because I am not a hand, I do not belong to the body," that would not make

it any less a part of the body. And if the ear should say, "Because I am not an eye, I do not belong to the body," that would not make it any less a part of the body. If the whole body were an eye, where would be the sense of hearing? If the whole body were an ear, where would be the sense of smell? But as it is, God arranged the members in the body, each one of them, as he chose. If all were a single member, where would the body be? As it is, there are many parts, yet one body. The eye cannot say to the hand, "I have no need of you," nor again the head to the feet, "I have no need of you." On the contrary, the parts of the body that seem to be weaker are indispensable, and on those parts of the body that we think less honorable we bestow the greater honor, and our unpresentable parts are treated with greater modesty, which our more presentable parts do not require. But God has so composed the body, giving greater honor to the part that lacked it, that there may be no division in the body, but that the members may have the same care for one another. If one member suffers, all suffer together; if one member is honored, all rejoice together. (1 Cor 12:12–26 ESV)

ONE MAIN THING

How many times have we looked at the gifts of someone in the church and felt insignificant? I struggle with not feeling like enough when I see my sweet sisters and how much they can accomplish. I don't feel needed when I am not called on to help with a large task or when I get left out of planning an event. It is then that we need to remind ourselves that we are part of the body. We are important.

Some of us will remember when we used to take communion on Sunday morning and put the cups in the holes in the back of the pew. Communion cups are not a big deal, right? What if the person in charge of clearing those cups left them for a week? What if they were left there for two weeks? All of a sudden, something that was not a big deal becomes a major problem. The person who takes care of those cups is a vital part of the body.

The Lord's church needs everyone to work together to seek and save the lost. My husband is a retired Navy Chief who got to spend some time aboard some big ships. When you are on a ship, everyone has a different job. Some are cooks, some are gunner's mates, some have jobs in the engine room, while others are mappers. Everyone does his or her job, and all things work well. When someone does not do his or her job, things get messy. Imagine how angry 200 men would be if the head cook took the day off because he didn't feel very appreciated. Imagine what might happen if the mappers decided not to plot the correct course because they just weren't feeling it that day.

GOING DEEPER

What does being part of the body of Christ mean? It means that you are part of something special. You may not have the gift of teaching, but you might be amazing at casseroles. You may not have the gift of evangelism, but you are the biggest encourager in the church. You are important. You are needed.

When we are part of the body of Christ, it means that Christ is our head. "And he put all things under his feet and gave him as head over all things to the church, which is his body, the fullness of him who fills all in all" (Eph 1:22–23). The word "body" in 1 Corinthians 12:12 is translated from *soma* in the original language. This same word is used for the physical body of Christ. This word is actually used over 140 times in the New Testament. Members of the body of Christ are the physical representation of Christ in this world. The church is the organism through which Christ manifests His life to the world today. We are the hands and feet of Jesus.

Members of the body of Christ are secure in their salvation.

 I give them eternal life, and they will never perish, and no one will snatch them out of my hand. My Father, who has given them to me, is greater than all, and no one is able to snatch them out of the Father's hand. I and the Father are one. (John 10:28–30)

For a Christian to lose his or her salvation, God would have to perform an "amputation" on the body of Christ!

When I was a little girl, I really believed that you spent the day going from "saved" to "unsaved." You would start off in the morning just fine. You had asked for forgiveness the night prior, so by the time you got to school, you were still among the saved. One little exaggeration or an eye roll and now all of a sudden you are lost for eternity. What a relief to understand that the blood of Christ continually cleanses us. "But if we walk in the light, as he is in the light, we have fellowship with one another, and the blood of Jesus his Son cleanses us from all sin" (1 John 1:7). The Greek word for "cleanses" is *katharizo*. This word is in the present tense here, which means it is continually happening. What a great feeling to know that, when we are walking in the light, we are continually being forgiven of our wrongdoings!

Members of the body of Christ share a common bond with all other Christians, regardless of background, race, or ministry. "There should be no division in the body, but ... ts parts should have equal concern for each other" (1 Cor 12:25). Church hurt is a real thing. When we are hurt by one of our family members in the Lord's church, that hurts worse than being hurt by people of the world. After all, these are the ones who should understand you and love you more than anyone else. We cannot lose sight of the fact that we are imperfect people worshiping with imperfect people. It is vital that we remember how much grace God has extended to us and that we do the same for others. A good rule is to extend grace to people as much as possible.

Members of the body of Christ share Christ's inheritance. "And if children, then heirs—heirs of God and fellow heirs with Christ, provided we suffer with him in order that we may also be glorified with him" (Rom 8:17). Inheritance and adoption were big deals in the Roman world. In the letter to Galatia, Paul let the people know that they too were part of the promise of Abraham (Gal 3). He says that they were, in fact, heirs to his promise, "that we might receive the adoption as sons" (Gal 4:5).

It would be enough that God purchases us out of the slave market. But He then adopts us to make us officially His. You do not adopt someone whom you do not truly love. It is a big process and takes a long time and a lot of money. Paul probably has in mind the Roman custom of adoption, where adopted sons were given absolutely equal privileges in the family and equal status as heirs.

Adoption was a crucial technique for sustaining the peculiarly Roman perspective on fathers and sons, in which every Roman was under the "paternal power" of the eldest male in the family. Adopted sons were *chosen* for the job and then assimilated into new families as natural sons.[1]

You can actually trace the lineage of powerful Roman leaders and see that almost all of them were adopted into a family as adults.

The Jews did not adopt very often. Their society was set up in such a way that if a woman were widowed, a family member would step in. Adoption was rarely necessary because the protection of their names and lineages precluded a child from becoming abandoned. Even though adoption wasn't a common practice for the first-century Jews, they had a good understanding of it. Adoptions in the ancient world usually consisted of a witness and a simple declaration, "You are my son." This also worked in reverse if a father wanted to disown his child.[2]

Members of the body of Christ receive the gift of Christ's righteousness. "For if, because of one man's trespass, death reigned through that one man, much more will those who receive the abundance of grace and the free gift of righteousness reign in life through the one man Jesus Christ" (Rom 5:17). Our own righteousness is not enough, but Christ's righteousness is more than enough.

WRAPPING IT UP

It is human to want to be loved and needed. As a teacher, I end every class by saying, "Know that you are loved." It is important to say that but also to show that. You do not have to be a great choral student to be loved in my class. You don't have to audition for a solo to be loved by me. You already are. Say it often, and show it often.

Something I see that happens in the body is that we get discouraged when our abilities become limited. As we age, we may have to cut back on some of the physical aspects of serving and think of other ways to serve.

I have heard stories of a lady in North Alabama years ago who had become very old. She was not able to get out anymore and felt her service for the Lord's church was limited. Instead of sitting at home lamenting her fate, she came up with a plan. She took out an ad in the local paper and published her phone number. The ad stated that you could call this lady at any time, and she would read the Bible to you. You could listen for as long as you wanted, and when you needed to, you could simply hang up. Even though her gifts were limited, she still was a vital part of the body. It is impossible to know how many lives were blessed by her reading God's word to complete strangers.

You are a big deal to Christ. It is fascinating to me to remember that Jesus does not need anything from us. There is nothing we can do for Him that will make His existence better. He does not need us, but He *wants* us. What a difference! Many times, we love others for what they can do for us, but Jesus's love transcends that. It does not matter what you think of your gifts—you are needed and wanted and loved.

PRAYER

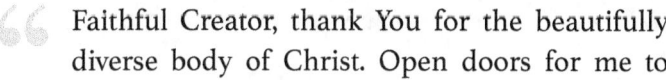 Faithful Creator, thank You for the beautifully diverse body of Christ. Open doors for me to

work together with my fellow Christians to be the hands and feet of Jesus as we submit to Him as our head. Remind me that no gift or role is insignificant and that every one of us is needed and essential to the church's mission.

FOUNDATIONAL QUESTIONS

1. How would people living during the time of the Bible have understood this metaphor in their historical and cultural context(s)?
2. How does God's choice of this metaphor help you better understand the way He views His people?
3. How does this metaphor enhance your understanding of the relationship between Christ and the church? Of your personal relationship with Jesus?
4. What does this metaphor help you learn about your *individual* role and *personal* responsibility as part of Christ's church?
5. How can the church as a *community* better embody this metaphor?
6. How might this metaphor help you explain the church to non-believers?
7. Are there any challenges that arise from misusing, misapplying, or over-emphasizing this metaphor?

GROUP DISCUSSION

1. What are some of the functions in the church that seem to get the most attention and appreciation? What roles seem to go unnoticed or be less valued?

2. How do feelings of insignificance or being overlooked affect members of the church? What can we do to make sure everyone feels valued and foster a sense of belonging?
3. The hand, ears, and mouth all have very different functions, yet each must perform those functions well to contribute to the overall health, and even existence, of the body. Discuss this concept of unity through diversity as it relates to the body of Christ.
4. How can understanding the interdependence of the body help us resolve conflict and promote unity within the church?
5. How can we each ensure we are actively contributing to the body in a way that aligns with our unique gifts and abilities?

*Consider providing a spiritual gifts assessment for individuals to complete. Follow up with a discussion on how each person can use his or her gifts to contribute to and improve the health of the body.

PERSONAL REFLECTION

1. Reflect on a time when a "small" part of the church body played a significant role in your life or the life of your congregation. How does this impact your understanding of community and the body of Christ?
2. Identify someone in your congregation who may feel overlooked or undervalued. Write a letter of encouragement to them, acknowledging and thanking them for their contribution or role.

3. Create a personal plan outlining how you can use your gifts and talents to serve the church over the next month or year. Include specific actions, such as visiting widows, painting a classroom, teaching a class, etc.

4

God's Building

Melissa McFerrin

ONE MAIN THING

THINKING OF OURSELVES AS A "BUILDING" is a bit challenging. The other chapters in this book, drawing on biblical metaphors, compare us to certain groups of people—priests, a family—or at least to living things—sheep, branches. But a building? As we will see, this description of God's people is saturated with deep significance that connects us to God's activity in the world throughout history, calls us to holier living, and gives us hope in eternity.

GOING DEEPER

To fully understand the significance of God's building, we need to trace some themes that run all the way through the Old and New Testaments. We'll start by going back—way back, to the 13th or 15th century BC, when the nation of Israel was learning how to follow the great God who had just delivered them from Egypt.

The Tabernacle

The tabernacle was the first building-like structure connected to God. (Before that there had been altars and monuments.) Shortly after the exodus, God commanded Moses to build Him a sanctuary to dwell in, giving minutely detailed instructions for its design (Exod 25:8–9 NASB 1995). When it was completed, "the cloud covered the tent of meeting, and the glory of the Lord filled the tabernacle" (Exod 40:34). This tent of meeting became the center of Israel's religious life in the wilderness, the place where the daily sacrifices were offered, where God spoke with Moses, and where atonement for sin was made (Exod 29:38–30:10). As long as Israel remained faithful, God promised, "I will make My dwelling among you, and My soul will not reject you. I will also walk among you and be your God, and you shall be My people" (Lev 26:11–12).

A tumultuous relationship followed wherein Israel failed to live up to the holiness God required, and God was forced to distance Himself from them (Deut 3:17–18). Eventually, Israel settled in the promised land. A more permanent building—the temple—was erected, and there was no more use for the tabernacle. We are not told what happened to it.

The tabernacle lived on in Israel's memory, however, and it does not disappear entirely from the pages of Scripture. During the divided-kingdom reigns of Uzziah (in Judah) and Jeroboam (in Israel), the prophet Amos recorded the Lord's intention to restore "the fallen booth" (Amos 9:11–12). In the midst of the exile, the Lord revealed to Ezekiel His plan to reunite the scattered descendants of Israel with one another and with their homeland. He echoed His own words from Leviticus: "[I] will set My sanctuary in their midst forever. My dwelling place also will be with them; and I will be their God, and they will be My people" (Ezek 37:26–27). The first fulfill-ment of this prophecy was the reestablishment of Israel in the promised land.

The Temple

Unlike the tabernacle, which originated with God, the temple was man's idea. After David was established as king, he purposed in his heart to build a magnificent house for the Lord. God's initial response was not favorable:

> You shall not build a house for Me to dwell in; for I have not dwelt in a house since the day that I brought up Israel to this day, but I have gone from tent to tent and from one dwelling place to another. In all places where I have walked with all Israel, have I spoken a word with any of the judges of Israel, whom I commanded to shep-herd My people, saying, "Why have you not built for Me a house of cedar?" (1 Chr 17:4–6)

God commended David for his sincere motives but post-poned construction until the peaceful reign of Solomon (1 Chr 22:7–10).

Solomon humbly acknowledged that nothing he designed, no matter how great, would be sufficient to contain God, whose dwelling place was in heaven (2 Chr 2:5–6; 6:18–21; see God's agreement in Isa 66:1–2). Solomon hoped the temple would serve as an earthly place to worship the name of the Lord. Still, at its dedication, the glory of the Lord descended from heaven with fire and filled the building (2 Chr 7:1–3)!

Solomon's temple stood as a symbol of Israel's (often waver-ing) allegiance to God for about 400 years before it was destroyed by the Babylonians during the siege of Jerusalem in 587–586 BC. God sent word through Zechariah that the exiles would return and rebuild it (Zech 6:12–13). As with the prophecy about the tabernacle, there are multiple layers to His statement, which we will investigate shortly. The second temple was completed in 515 BC (Ezra 6:14–15). Just before the time of Christ, Herod remodeled the temple to be the larger, grander one Jesus visited.

The House

The Hebrew noun translated "house" is an exceedingly common word that can refer to a physical habitation or to a family/household (among other meanings).[1] It shows up regularly in reference to the temple as the house of the Lord. But it's the idea of a family/household that we'll look at here because that usage is scattered throughout the history of God's people and is closely tied to predictions of a figurative "house" to come.

The priest Eli served just prior to a shift from priesthood to kingship as Israel's leadership model. After rebuking Eli for his sons' wickedness, God assured him that the priesthood would not disappear: "But I will raise up for Myself a faithful priest who will do according to what is in My heart and My soul; and I will build him an enduring house, and he will walk before My anointed always" (1 Sam 2:35). This may be referring in the short term to Zadok, who served under David.

Speaking of David, God had more to say when He responded to David's desire to build the temple. In a play on words, the Lord revealed that David would not build a house [structure] for Him, but

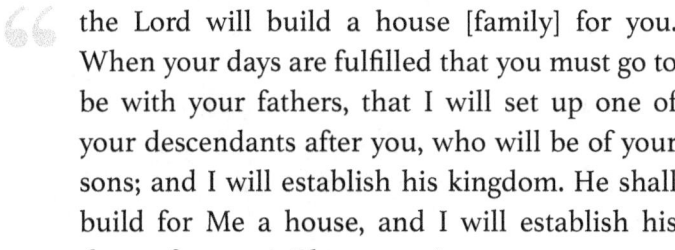

> the Lord will build a house [family] for you.
> When your days are fulfilled that you must go to
> be with your fathers, that I will set up one of
> your descendants after you, who will be of your
> sons; and I will establish his kingdom. He shall
> build for Me a house, and I will establish his
> throne forever. (1 Chr 17:10–12)

God had promised that a line of the priests would endure; here He promised the same for the kings. The coming king, of course, was Solomon—but the fulfillment didn't end with him.

You have probably figured out by now that this rich imagery in the Old Testament points forward, to One who would come and build a different type of tabernacle, temple, and house for the Lord. Let's see how it all comes together in Christ.

The Son

Upon observing the transfiguration, Peter suggested building three tabernacles—one each for Jesus, Moses, and Elijah (Luke 9:33). Keeping in mind what form the glory of the Lord took when He filled the original tabernacle, read carefully what happened next:

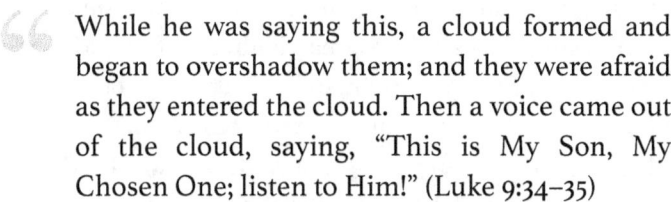

> While he was saying this, a cloud formed and
> began to overshadow them; and they were afraid
> as they entered the cloud. Then a voice came out
> of the cloud, saying, "This is My Son, My
> Chosen One; listen to Him!" (Luke 9:34–35)

In the first tabernacle, the Lord's presence appeared as a cloud. At the transfiguration, the Lord came again in a cloud! But this time He did not come to dwell; He came to accredit Jesus as His Son. An earthly tabernacle was not needed because God walked among them in the form of the incarnate Christ.

Jesus hinted at a similar idea in a conversation He had with the Jews early in His ministry. After rebuking those who were profaning the temple, Jesus stated that the temple would be destroyed, but He would raise it up in three days. The Jews questioned how He could so quickly restore an edifice that had taken decades to build. John reveals, "He was speaking of the temple of His body" (John 2:19–21). So, we see both the tabernacle and the temple connected to the person of Jesus.

What about the house, and God's promises to further the priestly line of Eli and the kingly line of David? We referenced Zechariah 6 when speaking of the post-exilic temple. That passage reads,

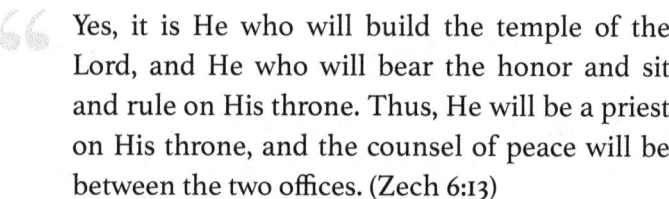

> Yes, it is He who will build the temple of the Lord, and He who will bear the honor and sit and rule on His throne. Thus, He will be a priest on His throne, and the counsel of peace will be between the two offices. (Zech 6:13)

Zechariah anticipated an alliance between the offices of priest and king. Jesus is the great high priest, not directly descended from Eli, but appointed by God (Heb 4:14–16; 7:14–22), and He also sits as the king, the son of David (Matt 21:9; 1 Tim 6:15). Hebrews 3:3–6 plainly states, "Christ was faithful as a Son over His house," the house which God built.

As far as a building for God's dwelling place, two orators in Acts (Stephen in Acts 7:46–50 and Paul in Acts 17:24–25) emphasize that God made the whole world, so He doesn't need a house built with human hands to live in. Since God is Spirit, He can be wherever He wants. Although He had the tabernacle crafted exactly how He wanted it, and although the temple was spectacular, neither was perfect. His throne is in heaven. But, since the time of the New Testament, He has also been abiding in something He considers better than a building, something He formed Himself—human beings.

The People

"We are the temple of the living God; just as God said, 'I will dwell in them and walk among them; and I will be their God, and they shall be My people'" (2 Cor 6:16). What an incredible honor! Not only did God choose us—followers of Christ—as His people, but He made us His habitation. He demonstrated this with the same kinds of signs He used with the first temple. Notice the parallels: At the temple's dedication, "fire came down from heaven ... and the glory of the Lord filled the house" (2 Chr 7:1). On the day of Pentecost,

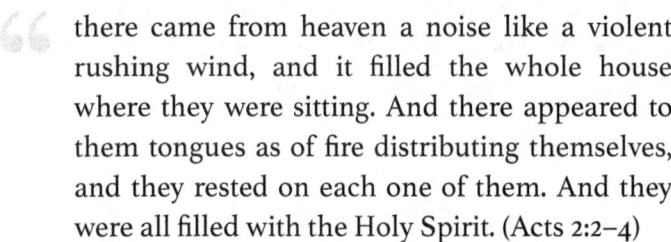

> there came from heaven a noise like a violent rushing wind, and it filled the whole house where they were sitting. And there appeared to them tongues as of fire distributing themselves, and they rested on each one of them. And they were all filled with the Holy Spirit. (Acts 2:2–4)

These special manifestations of the Lord were one-time events, but as He continued to associate with the temple, so He continues to be with us too.

Our status as the temple of God is a testament to the intimacy of the relationship we share, which was not possible before. The sacrifice of Christ tore open the veil of the physical temple, removing the barrier between the inner sanctuary of God and the rest of the building, where the priests worked (Matt 27:51). I assume you, like me, are not of Jewish descent, which means we started out with an even greater degree of separation (since Gentiles were not allowed anywhere in the temple complex). Interestingly, the early Christian leaders interpreted God's guarantee to "rebuild the tabernacle of David" not as a restoration of the Jewish religion, but as an indication "that the rest of mankind may seek the Lord, and all the Gentiles who are called by My name" (Acts 15:16–18; quoting Amos 9:11–12). Regardless of lineage, God has brought all of His people near, as near as can be.

There is still a very real element of danger and fear inherent in being in close contact with God (Heb 10:31). We must not treat this privilege lightly. His presence in us demands that we strive for holiness, as befits His temple (1 Cor 3:16–17). We are to glorify Him in our bodies (1 Cor 6:19–20). Just as God gave instructions about His buildings in the Old Testament, we have been given instructions on "how one ought to conduct himself in the household of God" today (1 Tim 3:15). We will never be perfect, but through our participation in His work in us, we can be pleasing to Him.

Looking Forward

The building motif does not end with the establishment of the church. Jesus encouraged His disciples with those famous words of hope concerning the dwelling places in His Father's house, His preparation for the disciples, and His eventual return to take them home (John 14:2–3). Paul reminded his readers,

> For we know that if the earthly tent which is our house is torn down, we have a building from God, a house not made with hands, eternal in the heavens. For indeed in this house we groan, longing to be clothed with our dwelling from heaven. (2 Cor 5:1–2)

Both Jesus and Paul were speaking of something to come. The faithful will experience one last building—or rather, an entire city, where they will remain in the dwelling place of God forever. "He who overcomes, I will make him a pillar in the temple of My God, and he will not go out from it anymore; and I will write on him the name of My God, and the name of the city of My God, the new Jerusalem, which comes down out of heaven from My God" (Rev 3:12).

Revelation 21 further describes this beautiful place. Of particular interest to us is verse 3, which should sound very familiar: "Behold, the tabernacle of God is among men, and He will dwell among them, and they shall be His people, and God Himself will be among them." Pay attention here. *The very same words that were first said about the tabernacle (Lev 26:11–12)—and then about the temple (Ezek 37:26–27)—and then about the church (2 Cor 6:16)—are also said about the heavenly city!* It will be the perfect, ultimate consummation of God's promise, repeated across thousands of years, to share Himself with the people He has claimed as His own in the place where He abides.

WRAPPING IT UP

We are still working toward that final, spiritual building. In the meantime, to help us remember who we are, we draw on Ephesians 2. Notice how it pulls together all our threads of thought.

> So then you are no longer strangers and aliens, but you are fellow citizens with the saints, and are of God's household [the house foretold in the Old Testament], having been built on the foundation of the apostles and prophets [who knew the temple and tabernacle], Christ Jesus Himself being the cornerstone [the embodiment of God among us], in whom the whole building, being fitted together, is growing into a holy temple in the Lord, in whom you also [the church now] are being built together into a dwelling of God in the Spirit [which will be fully realized in eternity]. (Eph 2:19–22)

Cherish the rich spiritual heritage of being God's building!

PRAYER

> Holy God, thank You for Your intimate presence in my life. Fill me with Your holiness, removing all impurities from my life. Thank You for sending Your Son and Your Spirit to show that You will always be with Your people. Strengthen me to contribute to building up Your church and never to be guilty of tearing it down. Live in and through me, oh my Lord and my God.

FOUNDATIONAL QUESTIONS

1. How would people living during the time of the Bible have understood this metaphor in their historical and cultural context(s)?
2. How does God's choice of this metaphor help you better understand the way He views His people?
3. How does this metaphor enhance your understanding of the relationship between Christ and the church? Of your personal relationship with Jesus?
4. What does this metaphor help you learn about your *individual* role and *personal* responsibility as part of Christ's church?
5. How can the church as a *community* better embody this metaphor?
6. How might this metaphor help you explain the church to non-believers?
7. Are there any challenges that arise from misusing, misapplying, or over-emphasizing this metaphor?

GROUP DISCUSSION

1. Why do you think God chose different types of "buildings" at different times in history? Compare His Old Testament dwellings to His dwelling now. What is the significance of the similarities and differences?
2. In light of how people experienced God's presence through His dwelling places, what does it mean for Him to dwell in us? How should this affect our view of the future?

3. We sing the song, "O Lord, prepare me to be a sanctuary... ." The tabernacle and temple were built by the hands of men, but we are formed by God to be His dwelling. What does that tell you about yourself and the church?
4. How can it be simultaneously true that the church is God's building, but He dwells in heaven, and the church hasn't yet arrived at heaven?
5. How should regarding our bodies as the temple of God affect our behavior and choices? How can we support each other in living this out?

PERSONAL REFLECTION

1. Does your identity as God's dwelling place bring you peace or make you uncomfortable? Why do you think that is?
2. What do you see as your role(s) in making God's building suitable for Him to dwell in?
3. Identify an area of your life that needs to grow in holiness. What guidance can you seek from other Christians? What habits or routines can you incorporate to foster that growth?

5

The Kingdom

Autumn Richardson

RECENTLY, I was able to check a most anticipated adventure off my bucket list. Picture it: London, June 2022. The crowds are pressing in around the Mall and the surrounding parks and streets, and it is still five hours until the big event. People have slept there to secure their spots, and those in the front (me!) keep getting smashed into the barricades by those in the back desperate to get just a glimpse. Some people are dressed in Union Jack dresses, hats, and t-shirts. Others have donned their dapper suits or best dresses and fancy hats. There are thousands of flags waving, and occasionally a small group of parade-goers burst into some British tune. Guards stand at attention every few yards along the route to ensure no one tries to breach the barricades. The press gathers in designated areas in their fanciest attire and seems just as excited as the commoners filling St. John's Park. When the parade finally begins, there are bands, war horses, bagpipers, and carriages in regal decor that march through the street for nearly an hour, followed by the main event: the royals. Trooping the Colour is an annual event that celebrates the birth and reign of the current monarch of Great Britain. It is planned for months and is a day of fanfare and celebration, tradition and honor. And most are there simply for a chance to wave at the royal family as they ride by in fancy carriages drawn by beautiful horses.

Now, picture it: the City of David, approximately 970 B.C. In 1 Kings 1, King David told his men to get his personal donkey and have Solomon ride it, taking along David's servants, to the Gihon Spring at the edge of the city. There, Zadok the priest and Nathan the prophet would anoint Solomon as king over Israel. This is in sharp contrast to Adonijah, who had just exalted himself as king in an act of defiance against David. He had thrown a parade and feast complete with cavalry and lavish sacrifices in the presence of royals and religious and military leaders. Yet, it was Solomon whom David and God chose as king and whose reign was to be greater than David's. The king God chose was not the likely, the obvious, or the most royal-looking option.

Fast-forward approximately a thousand years. When Jesus chose to formally announce His kingship to Jerusalem in the first century, He could have demanded a parade as lavish as Trooping the Colour. He could have exalted Himself and entered the city like Adonijah. He could have been carried in the finest chariot with war horses and thrown the largest feast Jerusalem had ever seen. He was, after all, to become the greatest king Israel had ever known. Yet, He chose the way of Solomon. He rode into Jerusalem on the back of a donkey, not a war horse. He came in with His disciples, not the scribes and Pharisees and priests. There was no great proclamation of His coming, only word of mouth that spread through the crowds, some of whom wanted to kill His friend Lazarus. What a different kind of king!

ONE MAIN THING

With so much imagery throughout Scripture that we'll only be able to scratch the surface, the church as the kingdom of God has been the source of much writing, theories, and even confusing doctrine. The idea that the kingdom is both "already" here and "not yet" fully realized is a paradox we wrestle to understand. Our Western minds struggle to see kingdoms as anything but the medieval picture of castles with moats, nobles, peasants, and knights. Yet, two things are clear: a kingdom is a realm where its monarch has absolute authority and rule, and the kingdom of God is unlike any earthly kingdom the world has ever seen.

GOING DEEPER

An Unlikely King

From His lowly birth to His death on the cross, nothing about the life of Jesus was regal. Kings are born in palaces with great fanfare. Jesus didn't even have a house (Matt 8:20). He was born in a stable with only shepherds to witness the angelic proclamation (Luke 2:1–20). Kings have heralds in the courts who enjoy the royal life as well. Jesus's primary heralds were Himself and John the Baptist, a man living in the wilderness like a prophet of old. Kings have subjects to serve them. Jesus came to serve His subjects (Matt 20:28). Kings are warriors with armies and weapons at their disposal. Jesus told His disciples not to fight (Matt 26:52; John 18:36). Kingly processions have great fanfare with war horses, chariots, and trumpets. Jesus entered Jerusalem on the back of a donkey that had never been ridden (Matt 21:1-11; cf. Zech 9:9–10).

Kings wear crowns of gold and jewels. Jesus wore a crown of thorns (Matt 27:29).

The Jews eagerly awaited a king, one of David's lineage, who would rescue them and restore them to their former glory. The prophets had painted a picture of a kingdom that would never be destroyed (Dan 2:44) and a Messiah who would bring peace and salvation to Israel (Isa 9:6–7; 52:7). When Jesus showed up on the scene claiming to be this expected One, those looking for earthly manifestations of the prophecies were sorely disappointed.

An Unlikely Kingdom

If the life Jesus lived was unusual for a king, the type of kingdom He proclaimed was even more so. The kingdom of God is often called an "upside-down kingdom" because it doesn't fit the norms of royalty in the first century or even today. Just as the Messiah chose to enter Jerusalem in an unexpected way, the nature of the kingdom also shocked the religious leaders and people eagerly awaiting His arrival.

Jesus claimed the kingdom was at hand (Mark 1:15), in their midst (Luke 17:21), and near (Luke 10:9), yet the people of Israel were still being ruled by the Roman government. So what is this kingdom, and who gets to be a part of it? The Sermon on the Mount is our first glimpse. Jesus used this opportunity "to unveil the nature of the kingdom and the nature of life in the kingdom."[1] It is here He announced the poor in spirit, mourners, peacemakers, and persecuted have a place in the kingdom (Matt 5:3–12). It is here He called His followers to a higher ethic than the letter of the Law (5:17–48). It is here He made clear that kingdom treasure is not physical (6:19–34). It is also here He cautioned that few will enter the kingdom (7:13–23).

Jesus continued His ministry by teaching values that oppose the world's view of power, authority, and glory. Those in His kingdom value humility over power, service over being served (Matt 23:11–12; John 13:1–17); childlikeness as greatness (Matt 18:3; 19:14); and laying one's life down rather than saving it (John 15:13). His parables about the kingdom's size, worth, and power (Matt 13) and those who are invited into it (18:23–35; 20:1–16; 22:2–14; 25:1–13) continued to stump the religious leaders and even His disciples.

Yet Jesus continued to proclaim the good news of the kingdom of God throughout His ministry. John the Baptist paved the way, but Jesus, though king, was also herald of His kingdom. Most of the time when the Gospels mention Jesus as "proclaiming," they also mention Him as calling people to repentance (Mark 1:14–15) or performing acts of mercy (Matt 4:23; 9:35; Luke 8:1). And when He sent His apostles out to carry on His mission, He instructed them to do the same (Luke 9:2). Perhaps this is why Paul says in 1 Corinthians 4:20 that the kingdom is not a matter of talk, but of power.

The Church As the Kingdom

When we think of kingdoms, we think of geographic realms, like the ancient Roman Empire or the United Kingdom. Jesus's kingdom, however, is not a territory, but simply His rule or His authority. His reign is not of this world, and His fight is not against the physical powers of this world. Instead, Jesus reigns over His people, the church, and is defeating the enemies of death and sin (1 Cor 15:24–27). After His personal resurrection and victory over death, He proclaimed His ultimate authority once more and passed on the job of heralding to His disciples (Matt 28:18–20). As part of His kingdom, we are citizens of heaven (Phil 3:20) and ambassadors seeking to expand His rule (2 Cor 5:19–21) through proclaiming the kingdom the way He did—calling people to repentance and doing acts of mercy.

Entry into this glorious kingdom is not bound by territory, location, nationality, or any other physical demarcation. In fact, 1 Corinthians 15:50 makes it clear that flesh and blood have no place in the kingdom. Therefore, those who live by the flesh, or unrighteousness, cannot inherit it (1 Cor 6:9–10; Gal 5:19–21; Eph 5:5). Access to the reign of Christ is free to all (Gal 3:28) who are willing to be delivered from the domain of darkness (Col 1:13) and be born of water and the Spirit (John 3:3–5; Acts 8:12).

What is our response to this deliverance into the kingdom of light? Gratefulness, worship, and reverence (Heb 12:28). Citizens of the kingdom of God must also live differently than citizens of the world. Below is a list of New Testament references that lay out who is part of, or will ultimately inherit, the kingdom:

- Those who serve the hungry, sick, and imprisoned (Matt 25:34–36)
- The poor in spirit (Matt 5:3)
- The persecuted (Matt 5:10)
- Those whose righteousness exceeds that of the Scribes and Pharisees (Matt 5:19–20)
- Those who do the will of the Father (Matt 7:21)
- Those who are humble like little children (Matt 18:3; 19:14; Mark 10:15)
- Those who forgive (Matt 18:21–35)
- Those who serve (Matt 20:1–28)
- The fruitful (Matt 21:43)
- Those judged worthy for their suffering (2 Thess 1:5; Rom 8:17)

- Those who partake of the divine nature to make their calling sure (2 Pet 1:3–11)

All of these qualities are qualities of Christ Himself. They are the qualities of One who would ride into town on a donkey, humbly, instead of on a war horse, seeking attention and fame. We, as His kingdom, are to be like Him, act like Him, live like Him, and eventually rule with Him (Rev 22:3–5) when the ultimate fulfillment of the kingdom comes.

WRAPPING IT UP

When we look at the physical authorities in our lives, we see imperfection at best, but often corruption and constant struggles over power. This can be unsettling and make us anxious about our futures. Yet, it was the Father's "good pleasure" to give us His kingdom (Luke 12:32 ESV), prepared for us before the foundation of the world (Matt 25:34). We are citizens and co-heirs of that better kingdom, subjects of a perfect King, and called to a higher purpose that embodies values the world often opposes. The kingdom of God is one of power (1 Cor 4:20; Mark 9:1) that cannot be shaken (Heb 12:28), as foretold in the Old Testament. It is not physical, but "righteousness, peace, and joy" (Rom 14:17). The church serves as "an outpost of the kingdom of God now, a community already living under the rule of God in accordance with the ethic Jesus established, looking forward to inheriting the kingdom (Matt 25:34; Rom 8:17; cf. 1 Cor 6:9; 15:50) at the consummation of all things."[2] Let us therefore "seek first the kingdom of God and His righteousness" (Matt 6:33) and proclaim its good news as we live among the kingdoms of men as "strangers and temporary residents" (1 Pet 2:11).

PRAYER

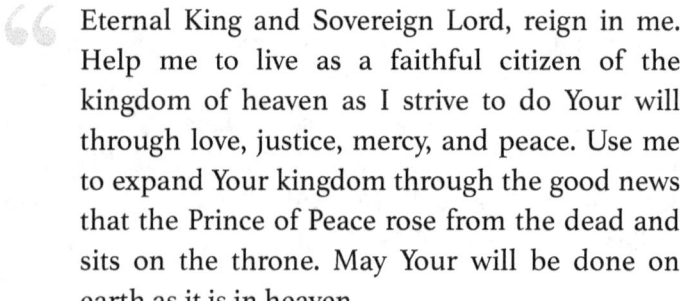 Eternal King and Sovereign Lord, reign in me. Help me to live as a faithful citizen of the kingdom of heaven as I strive to do Your will through love, justice, mercy, and peace. Use me to expand Your kingdom through the good news that the Prince of Peace rose from the dead and sits on the throne. May Your will be done on earth as it is in heaven.

FOUNDATIONAL QUESTIONS

1. How would people living during the time of the Bible have understood this metaphor in their historical and cultural context(s)?
2. How does God's choice of this metaphor help you better understand the way He views His people?
3. How does this metaphor enhance your understanding of the relationship between Christ and the church? Of your personal relationship with Jesus?
4. What does this metaphor help you learn about your *individual* role and *personal* responsibility as part of Christ's church?
5. How can the church as a *community* better embody this metaphor?
6. How might this metaphor help you explain the church to non-believers?
7. Are there any challenges that arise from misusing, misapplying, or over-emphasizing this metaphor?

GROUP DISCUSSION

1. What is the relationship between the church as the present expression of the kingdom of God and the kingdom's future consummation? What is it like to live in this tension of "already but not yet"?
2. Discuss struggles you have experienced as citizens of a spiritual kingdom living in a physical one.
3. Matthew 6:19–34 discusses the battle to focus on material things versus spiritual things. What does it look like to seek first the kingdom of God (v. 33) in our personal decisions and priorities?
4. Matthew 25 lists six categories of people that those invited into the kingdom served. How can we seek out each of these populations and minister to them?
5. If proclaiming or heralding is a primary mission of the kingdom, how can we better equip and encourage each other in this responsibility?

PERSONAL REFLECTION

1. How can I align my everyday actions more with the ethics of God's kingdom, such as peace, justice, humility, and righteousness?
2. In what areas of my life do I not always allow God to be King? How can I more fully surrender to His Lordship?
3. Look at Scriptures that list actions or attitudes that can keep us from inheriting the kingdom of God. Choose one that you actively struggle with and determine how you will better fight against it in the coming weeks.

6

A Royal Priesthood

Carol Sparks

But ye are a chosen generation, *a royal priesthood*, an holy nation, a peculiar people; that ye should shew forth the praises of him who hath called you out of darkness into his marvellous light: Which in time past were not a people, but are now the people of God: which had not obtained mercy, but now have obtained mercy. (1 Pet 2:9–10 KJV, emphasis added)

HAVE you ever watched the British royal family? Do you love the pomp and circumstance, the majestic ceremony accompanying them? Most little girls want to be princesses at some point in their childhood. The pageantry of royalty is heady, but being royalty also carries immense responsibility.

ONE MAIN THING

When I thought about a royal priesthood, the word "royal" had me scratching my head. What exactly did that mean? Merriam-Webster defines it as being "of kingly ancestry; of, relating to, or subject to the crown; being in the crown's service."[1] Christians meet all of these criteria:

- We are children of the King (John 1:12).
- We are subject to the King (John 14:23).
- We are in the King's service (Deut 10:12).

Being royalty is about our relationship with the King. This royalty is not earned or deserved; it is made available to all people willing to become children of God. It is a special status that shows our closeness to our King. Because of that special status, we also enjoy great blessings and benefits. We are both welcomed and encouraged to come before God's throne without fear to request help. Our King is not like the king in the book of Esther. Esther could have been put to death for approaching her husband, the king, without an invitation. Can you imagine how terrified this young woman must have been? Can you feel her relief when he held out his scepter to her? We never have to experience that fear when we seek help from our Father, the King of the universe.

Allow me to share a personal anecdote. Years ago, my father was a teacher at my high school. He was known for his strict but fair approach. Most students viewed him with a lot of respect and a smidgen of fear. One day, I was upset over a problem, as high schoolers often are. I asked to talk to my father. Because I was Mr. Wilhite's daughter, I was given unusual permission to leave class to go to Dad's classroom. A couple of teachers stopped me in the hallway, but when they realized to whom I belonged, they allowed me to continue. When I appeared in the doorway of Dad's room, he immediately stopped his lesson and came to me to set my world back in its proper place. There was no fussing, no anger, just loving concern. His steadfast love for his child made such a deep impression on me that I still remember it vividly a gazillion years later. Being Mr. Wilhite's daughter gave me rights, blessings, and recognition I had not earned. That is a mere shadow of what it means to be a child of the King of kings. As children of the King, we are not just loved, but we also receive His rights, blessings, and recognition that we have not earned.

Now, let's turn our attention to the second word—priesthood. The term "priesthood" describes our unique role given to us by God. Merriam-Webster defines a priest as "someone who is authorized to perform the sacred rites of a religion especially as a mediatory agent between humans and God."[2] As priests, we mediate between God and a world that has lost its way. Through us, the lost world can be reconciled to God. Some scholars stress that the role of the priest is paramount in this metaphor; others suggest that the unity aspect is. Our initiation (baptism) into the priesthood changes us from individual people to a nation.[3] First Peter 2:10 tells us that in the past, we were not a people, but now we are. The nation of God's people shares a common bond and purpose. Put simply, our purpose is to bring the lost to God's kingdom. We teach not only with words, but also with our actions.

Let's briefly look at what the royal priesthood is not. It is not only for men. In some congregations today, women are almost a secondary class of Christians; the focus is on what women cannot do. When I was growing up, the message for girls was to be a wife, a mother, and a Sunday School teacher. While these are all excellent, they should not be the totality of our Christian responsibilities. Recently, I heard a sermon from a popular brotherhood minister on raising sons and daughters to be faithful Christians. He spent ten minutes on the many jobs and roles their sons should aspire toward. It gave parents hope about what lies ahead for their sons.

Parents were anticipating a similar list of roles and jobs that would encourage and motivate their daughters toward greater service. The total list for their daughters was Sunday School teachers. Please do not misunderstand; being a Sunday School teacher is a great responsibility and blessing, but it is not the sum of what women are to do as members of the royal priesthood. Most commands given to Christians are equally applicable to men and women. Because of who we are and who we belong to, let's go out and do what God expects!

GOING DEEPER

In today's world, most people see royalty as an elite class. They are special, so they must be better than everyone else. Because royalty (and the "elite") are seen as better than others, it is no surprise that many are haughty, arrogant, and just plain snooty. Look no further than Hollywood and Washington, D.C., for examples of this mindset. We use words today like "entitled," "elite," or "Karens" to convey our dislike of this attitude. Christians are indeed a special people, but we must not allow an arrogant attitude to take root in our nation of royal priests. I love the KJV's use of "a peculiar people" in 1 Peter 2:10. "Peculiar" here does not mean strange or odd; it denotes a people who are God's cherished treasure or God's own possession. This is the same terminology used in the Old Testament to describe the relationship between God and His chosen people, Israel. Like the children of Israel, we are set apart to fill a special role.

As the royal priesthood, God's peculiar people, are we better than others? Do we enjoy an elite status? Yes and no. We derive our specialness solely from our relationship with God, so in that regard, we are part of a blessed group of people.

God has given us an immeasurable value that we do not earn nor deserve. But does God love us more? Christ (God) loved everyone enough to endure humiliation and death in their place. We understand that God loves and values everyone when we learn to see others through God's eyes. Jewish rabbis use the following illustration to help us see others as God sees them: The name of God in Hebrew is Yahweh (יהוה).

If you spell Yahweh vertically instead of right to left, the letters form the stick figure of a man, with a head, shoulders with arms, a torso, and hips with legs. Whenever you look at another human being, you can see the name of God in their form. This should remind us that this is a person made in the image of God and greatly loved by God.[4] Are we more valuable than they? No. Does God love us more? No. Do we have a close relationship with God Almighty that others do not have? Yes!

The royal priesthood is a holy nation. In this context, "nation" means much more than living in the same geographical country. It is a group of people who are joined by relationships, purposes, and goals. We are a community. Since the introduction of the smartphone and the explosion of social media, people have become more isolated than ever. Add the recent pandemic with its lockdowns, and it is no wonder that depression and anxiety are at high levels. People are no longer a part of a true community. The Wall Street Journal recently ran an article linking the increase in depression with the decrease in going to church.[5] Another Wall Street Journal article published a few days after the first article reported on a growing trend of Americans returning to church so they can be part of a community.[6] Isn't it ironic that America had to take such a long, torturous path to realize that God was right all along? Like a light that shines the brightest in the dark, we have an incredible opportunity to show the world what a true community looks like.

In Luke 4:16–21, we read the account of Jesus reading from Isaiah 61 at the synagogue. He informed the assembly that this saying was fulfilled in their hearing. Isaiah 61 is what I like to call the "Beauty for Ashes" chapter. It tells how the wrongs will be made right, justice will come, and there will be beauty for ashes when the day of the Lord comes. Isaiah 61:6 (ESV) reads, "But you shall be called the priests of the Lord; they shall speak of you as the ministers of our God." In effect, we, as the royal priests, are the intermediaries that God uses to right the wrongs, bring justice to the downtrodden, and heal the sick.

We are all familiar with the story of the Good Samaritan. A Jewish man was waylaid by thieves, robbed, beaten, and left for dead. The priest and the Levite passed by on the other side of the road, declining to help the Jewish man lying in the ditch. We don't know why they refused to help; perhaps they were late for their duties at the temple or felt too holy to deal with the messiness of a bloodied man. Maybe they thought the man deserved what he got, a foolish man traveling that dangerous road alone! Whatever excuse they had for failing to help, they did not get their hands dirty. On the other hand, the royal priesthood wades into the messiness of life to bring comfort and healing to everyone they can.

WRAPPING IT UP

Who are we? We are a royal priesthood, a holy nation, and a peculiar people. As such, we have a close relationship with the Creator of the universe. We can approach our Father without fear and obtain help in times of need. We have been set apart for a particular purpose—"that ye should shew forth the praises of him who hath called you out of darkness into his marvellous light" (1 Pet 2:9 KJV). Because we have been shown such great love, we, in turn, must perform our priestly duties with great love. To me, the saddest words in the entire Bible are found in 1 Corinthians 13:1–3 (ESV):

> If I speak in the tongues of men and of angels, but have not love, I am a noisy gong or a clanging cymbal. And if I have prophetic powers, and understand all mysteries and all knowledge, and if I have all faith, so as to remove mountains, but have not love, I am nothing. If I give away all I have, and if I deliver up my body to be burned, but have not love, I gain nothing.

How heartbreaking to do all the right things but lose everything in the end because there was no love.

In conclusion, our special designation as royal priests is not because we are righteous or superior to others. Instead, it is because God loves us enough to provide a way to be reconciled with Him. By becoming Christians, we have accepted our purpose of mediating between God and an evil world. Let's go out and see people as God sees them. Let's do what needs to be done to help others reconcile with God. Most importantly, let's ensure we operate from a place of love since loving others is the most visible sign of our love for God. May our love for God shine as a beacon of hope to a dark and miserable world. Let's go and get our hands dirty to lead as many souls as possible into the kingdom of light and the community of royal priests.

PRAYER

> Righteous God, thank You for honoring me with a place in Your royal priesthood. Enable me to come before Your throne without fear, knowing Your love provides a way for us to be reconciled with You. Allow me to see others as You see them and to become a mediator so they may experience Your love, kindness, and forgiveness.

FOUNDATIONAL QUESTIONS

1. How would people living during the time of the Bible have understood this metaphor in their historical and cultural context(s)?

2. How does God's choice of this metaphor help you better understand the way He views His people?
3. How does this metaphor enhance your understanding of the relationship between Christ and the church? Of your personal relationship with Jesus?
4. What does this metaphor help you learn about your *individual* role and *personal* responsibility as part of Christ's church?
5. How can the church as a *community* better embody this metaphor?
6. How might this metaphor help you explain the church to non-believers?
7. Are there any challenges that arise from misusing, misapplying, or over-emphasizing this metaphor?

GROUP DISCUSSION

1. In what ways can we ensure we do not develop arrogant attitudes in our "elite" position as a royal priesthood of God?
2. What impact does our being holy and "peculiar people" have on our interactions with the world? How is this at tension with our role as priestly mediators between God and people?
3. Thinking of the diverse responsibilities of priesthood, how can we better identify, value, and uplift the roles of everyone in the church, regardless of age or gender?
4. Discuss how an absence of love can undermine our ministry efforts, and identify steps we can take to present a genuine, love-driven approach to service.

5. What are some practical ways we can avoid the pitfalls of the Levite and priest in the parable of the Good Samaritan and willingly wade into the "messiness" of others' lives to bring comfort and healing?

PERSONAL REFLECTION

1. How can confidence to approach God's throne without fear transform the way you pray?
2. How do you handle feelings of inadequacy or unworthiness in light of being part of God's royal priesthood? What are some Scriptures that can help you see yourself as God sees you?
3. Can you think of a time when being part of a "peculiar people" was uncomfortable for you? How did you handle that situation? What are some ways you can stand out in a positive way in your daily interactions?

7

Branches on the Vine

Molly Daily

ONE MAIN THING

EVER WONDER why so many metaphors in the Bible revolve around nature and plants? Ever noticed how many parables talk about gardening? Many civilizations of biblical times were accustomed to agricultural practices. People knew and understood the life cycle of plants. They could identify the basic structures of different plants and what jobs those structures hold in ensuring the growth, survival, and reproduction of the plants.

One particular type of plant mentioned throughout the Bible is a vine and its branches. The vine is used as a symbol of life, growth, and fertility—a promise of wealth for future generations. God's actions toward His favored people are compared to those of a vinedresser. In Psalm 80:8–11, we read,

> You brought a vine out of Egypt; you drove out the nations and planted it. You cleared the ground for it; it took deep root and filled the

land. The mountains were covered with its shade, the mighty cedars with its branches; it sent out its branches to the sea, and its shoots to the River. (NRSV)

However, we also see a warning that if God's people, the branches, do not absorb the goodness of the vine's nutrients, then they can ultimately succumb to blight, disease, and barrenness. "When I wanted to gather them, says the Lord, there are no grapes on the vine, nor figs on the fig tree; even the leaves are withered, and what I gave them has passed away from them" (Jer 8:13).

To better understand the metaphors based on a vine and its branches, we first need to understand the basic biological structures and functions of the plant itself.[1] The vine is the sustainer of life; the branches are its offspring. The vine is what is connected to the ground, to the minerals, to the vitamins. The vine funnels these nutrients to the branches so that they can bloom and produce fruit. Simply put, the branches rely on the vine. If the branches were to be severed from the vine, they would have no means of survival. Likewise, the vine depends on the branches. The sprouts, or branches, develop the leaves. The leaves are where photosynthesis occurs, which in turn gives the vine the stamina to thrive and yield fruit. The tendrils that the branches generate are the fingers that pull and stretch the vine to areas of optimal sunlight.

Pruning, or cutting off the dead branches, boosts the growth of the vine by allowing it to focus its nutrients on bud growth instead of wasting essential minerals and vitamins on defunct offshoots. The young, tender branches eventually thicken into mature extensions of the vine, begetting future harvests.

GOING DEEPER

Close your eyes for just a moment and think of spring. What words or images pop into your head? "Green," "lush," "beginnings," and "renewal" are just a few. So many people look forward to spring because of the regeneration of the land—the buds, the blooms—an assurance of new growth and promising yields. Have you ever grown a fruit-producing plant in your yard? If you have, you'll know that the flowers are what ultimately become the fruit. How can we, as Christians, expect to bear fruit for His kingdom, His church, if we do not first produce flourishing blooms?

In John 15:1–5, Jesus states,

> I am the true vine, and my Father is the vine-grower. He removes every branch in me that bears no fruit. Every branch that bears fruit he prunes to make it bear more fruit. You have already been cleansed by the word that I have spoken to you. Abide in me as I abide in you. Just as the branch cannot bear fruit by itself unless it abides in the vine, neither can you unless you abide in me. I am the vine, you are the branches. Those who abide in me and I in them bear much fruit, because apart from me you can do nothing.

Just as the branches are the offspring of the vine, so are we the offspring of the Lord. He sustains and supplies us with what we need to produce the fruit of His kingdom. When we take what we have learned from the word of God and apply it to our lives, we are absorbing the nutrients that are necessary to grow as His people, His branches. This growth will encourage the development of fruit—bringing others into His fold through the sharing of His word, His grace, and His goodness. If we, as the branches, do not consume these nutrients, we will neither sprout nor produce fruit, and if we separate ourselves from the life-giving vine, our branches will become barren.

Sometimes we think He prunes the barren branches, but that is not exactly what John 5:2 suggests. He *removes* the branches that bear no fruit. There is a short, four-verse parable in Luke 13 about a fig tree that does not produce figs. After three years with no fruit, the owner tells the gardener to cut it down, but the gardener asks for one more year, in which he plans to care for it more diligently—digging and fertilizing—to promote growth. There are lessons in this parable about God's forgiveness and grace, and maybe His patience with the nation of Israel, but the practical point for us is there are things we can do in faith to promote growth in our lives. Through study, prayer, and practicing other spiritual disciplines, we can water and fertilize our hearts and ask God to give the increase. Through an active faith that serves others and God, we can live more fruitfully for Him.

On the other hand, pruning is a different process! After a prolonged freeze a couple of winters ago, a Christian sister's camellia bushes looked dead; they had few leaves and no flowers the following winter. But the plants weren't actually dead. The following spring a few leaves sprouted, and she pruned the shrubs back, way back. They didn't look great at first, but the cutting back promoted growth so the roots could nourish the branches and the shrubs could flourish once again. John 15:2 says, "Every branch that bears fruit he prunes to make it bear more fruit." This pruning process is not a sign of deadness or barrenness, but actually an indication of fruitfulness. The process can be painful and is not always pretty or comfortable, but the end result is more leaves, more flowers, more fruit. The end result is growth. What seems like painful pruning in our lives may actually be God's way of making us more productive, so we trust Him—Scripture says we "abide" in Him—to make the cuts necessary to accomplish the work He is about in our lives.

Christians can go through seasons just as nature does—seasons of dormancy and seasons of growth. Sometimes we will need to look for ways to dig and fertilize our spiritual lives to encourage flourishing. At times we will need to encourage new growth by pruning, cutting off that which is hindering us. These hindrances may be bad habits, addictions, or seemingly simple pastimes that keep us from spending time in His word and with His church. Other times, our unfruitfulness is a matter of laziness or simple unproductiveness. After all, growth is an active process. By not participating in this process, we are extinguishing the nutrient supply to our branches. If we are not mindful of this, we put ourselves in a situation that demands pruning to ensure future growth. Even though it is normal to go through seasons of dormancy, we should always desire and welcome seasons of growth.

WRAPPING IT UP

How can we be the branches that God needs to keep His vine healthy and robust? We need to be the extension of Him and His church, just as branches are the extensions of the vine. We need to bring the beauty of God's love to the world, like when spring ushers in the loveliness of an awakening season. A simple smile or a kind word can go a long way. Will this bring growth to the church right away? Not necessarily. However, it can prepare the soil so the seed can be planted.

Does a vine grow, sprout, flower, and produce fruit in a matter of days? Absolutely not. It takes time, nurturing, tending.

Get to know a colleague at work. Encourage others with a positive attitude—some sunshine for their day. Over time, that colleague will hopefully come to realize that there is something that sets you apart from others—something that they may be interested in knowing more about. This leads to sharing Jesus. It might also present you with an opportunity to invite that colleague to church or to sit down with them and tell them more about what it means to be part of God's family. They will see in you the joy described in John 15:11 and want to experience joy and other fruit of the Spirit (Gal 5) they see in your life.

Are you a Christian who is ripe in your faith and who has been active in the church for years? Take time to encourage those who are young in the faith. Reach out to them when they are struggling. Be a shoulder to cry on, an ear to listen. It is very possible that they want you to share your wisdom and your advice but do not know how to ask for it. Investing in the lives of those younger in the faith will encourage high-yielding harvests for the future church.

Do you feel like you may have a spiritual "brown thumb," with little or no good growth in your life? Spend time developing or deepening your relationship with God. After all, He is the giver of life. He is the one who supplies us with the nutrients that we need to grow as Christians. If we have no connection to the vine, we will wither and dry up. Push yourself to grow and to become active in your congregation. You cannot provide an abundant garden for the Lord if you have not tilled and fertilized your own soil first.

Are you going through a time of pruning, a painful but essential part of the growth process? In our spiritual lives, pruning might come in the form of trials, temptation, challenges, or constructive criticism. It might require us to eliminate bad habits or relationships. These experiences remove parts of our lives that hinder our growth and make us more fruitful in the long run.

There are many factors that contribute to successful growth, but the process can be a slow one. In a world where so many people, businesses, and devices offer us instant gratification, we can forget that growing a true, strong foundation takes time and dedication. Our spiritual lives require attention, tending, and nurturing. At times, this may be difficult, but His promise in John 15:5, 7–11 remains true, and the resulting joy is worth the effort:

> I am the vine, you are the branches. Those who abide in me and I in them bear much fruit, because apart from me you can do nothing. ... If you abide in me, and my words abide in you, ask for whatever you wish, and it will be done for you. My Father is glorified by this, that you bear much fruit and become my disciples. As the Father has loved me, so I have loved you; abide in my love. If you keep my commandments, you will abide in my love, just as I have kept my Father's commandments and abide in his love. I have said these things to you so that my joy may be in you, and that your joy may be complete.

Like the branches described in these passages, we are dependent on God for everything we need for life, and our intentional nurturing of our spiritual life will lead to increased growth in our lives and in the kingdom of God. Ultimately, this fruit will honor Him, attract the notice of others in our life, and give Him the glory for the work He is doing.

PRAYER

 Lord, keep me connected to You always. Help me to draw my strength, sustenance, and nourishment from You so that I may grow and bear fruit. Prune me when there are sins or distractions present in my life. Enable the fruit I bear to glorify and bring honor to Your name.

FOUNDATIONAL QUESTIONS

1. How would people living during the time of the Bible have understood this metaphor in their historical and cultural context(s)?
2. How does God's choice of this metaphor help you better understand the way He views His people?
3. How does this metaphor enhance your understanding of the relationship between Christ and the church? Of your personal relationship with Jesus?
4. What does this metaphor help you learn about your *individual* role and *personal* responsibility as part of Christ's church?
5. How can the church as a *community* better embody this metaphor?
6. How might this metaphor help you explain the church to non-believers?
7. Are there any challenges that arise from misusing, misapplying, or over-emphasizing this metaphor?

GROUP DISCUSSION

1. What are some of the spiritual nutrients we rely on to sustain our growth? What happens when we don't access those regularly?
2. What kinds of things hinder growth, cause disease, or cause us to wilt on the vine?
3. Christians go through seasons just like plants—times of dormancy, times of growth, and times of bearing fruit. How can we best support each other in those different seasons?
4. What kinds of fruit should we bear for Christ, individually and collectively?
5. How can we foster a spiritually nourishing environment, much like a greenhouse for plants, so our people can grow and bear fruit?

PERSONAL REFLECTION

1. What habits, practices, or relationships make you feel most connected to the vine? Are there ways that you feel disconnected?
2. Think of a time of pruning in your life. How did this help you grow? Is there anything currently in your life that is hindering growth and needs to be pruned?
3. Think of someone in your spiritual community who seems dormant or disconnected from the vine. How can you help provide that person with spiritual nourishment?

8

The Flock

Cayron Mann

THERE IS a story about a couple who received word that their baby boy, whom they were adopting, was about to be born. After arriving at the hospital, the couple eagerly peered through the massive nursery window, wondering which newborn was "theirs." A nurse, who had been watching for them, gestured for the couple to enter through a side door.

No wonder they had not seen him at the display window! There he was, at the back, leisurely soaking up the blue ultraviolet light that is routinely used to treat jaundice in newborns.

Elated, the couple was allowed to spend a few minutes with him, holding and feeding and just staring at him before visiting hours ended for the night. Although it was late, they cherished that brief introduction.

The next day, the birth family spent valuable time with him as they loved on him and prayed and shared their hopes for his future.

On the day of his discharge from the hospital, the adoptive parents learned that they were finally going to be alone with him in a hospital room and have that unique time together as a new family.

They waited in the hallway as the nurse wheeled the bassinet toward them, and they gazed at the precious sleeping face of the infant lying there.

A sudden uneasiness came over this new mom. She tried to dismiss it, yet, as mothers know, a nagging thought doesn't just go away. "Surely not," she wondered. Something wasn't quite right. She decided to voice her concern and said with a timid smile, "Maybe it's me, but that just doesn't look like him." The nurse laughed a gentle, reassuring laugh.

"Of course," the mother continued nervously, "I've also read that infants can change a lot in those first few days."

She looked deeper into the infant's face, and hesitated, "I know it sounds crazy, but something seems different." Not wanting to create additional tension and in order to ease the mother's mind, the nurse stopped and offered to take a moment to adjust the bassinet and check over the infant's coloring and appearance. "Let's also make sure of a fresh diaper change," she suggested kindly.

During those quick seconds of the diaper change, the nurse's facial expression changed into one of surprise and embarrassed amusement. With a smile, she said to the mother, "You're right—you know your baby. This is a girl! I'll be right back!" And, within seconds, the nurse brought their son whom they had met just two days earlier.

The reality set in. This mother, although she had spent barely an hour with him, knew him. She recognized his face. She knew her son.

ONE MAIN THING

For a moment, consider these verses from John 10:1–5 (ESV):

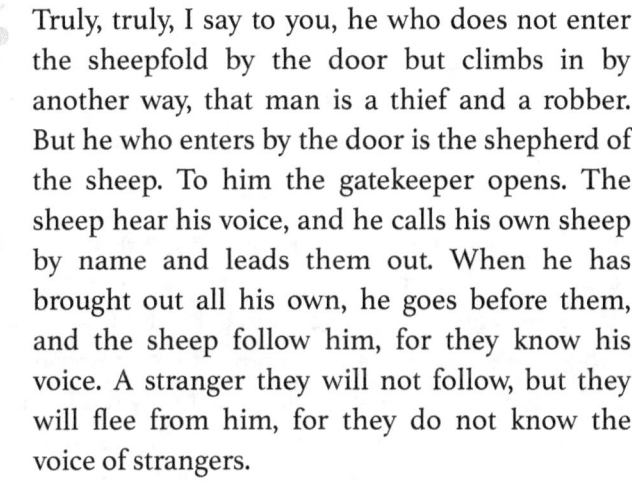

> Truly, truly, I say to you, he who does not enter the sheepfold by the door but climbs in by another way, that man is a thief and a robber. But he who enters by the door is the shepherd of the sheep. To him the gatekeeper opens. The sheep hear his voice, and he calls his own sheep by name and leads them out. When he has brought out all his own, he goes before them, and the sheep follow him, for they know his voice. A stranger they will not follow, but they will flee from him, for they do not know the voice of strangers.

Scripture often uses the metaphor of comparing Christians to sheep. Think about it. We exhibit qualities of sheep in three distinct ways:

- We are preyed upon by the enemy.
- We will become lost when we stray from the flock.
- We must be led back by a shepherd (we cannot do it on our own).

Jesus proclaims Himself the Good Shepherd in many ways (guiding, nurturing, protecting), yet the most distinctive way is that He clearly states, "I am the good shepherd. The good shepherd lays down his life for the sheep" (John 10:11). Paul reminds us of the matchless love of Jesus in Romans 5:6–8: "For while we were still weak, at the right time Christ died for the ungodly. For one will scarcely die for a righteous person —though perhaps for a good person one would dare even to die—but God shows his love for us in that while we were still sinners, Christ died for us." It wasn't when we became "good enough," and it wasn't when we achieved perfection. It was when we were lost. Vulnerable. Deep in the depths of sin. His dying on the cross and overcoming death by rising from the tomb covers us when we have gone astray and cannot find our way back on our own. He comes looking for us, because He was ready and willing to lay down His life so that we can return to the flock again and again.

In 2019, three-year-old Ashton Schultz fell over a bridge into Detroit Lake on Father's Day. Immediately his father, Chris, leapt into the water. He struggled to get Ashton to someone near the shore but was then unable to stay above water himself. Ashton was pulled to safety. Not only did Chris give the ultimate sacrifice of his life for his son, it was soon found out that he was also an organ donor, and, in his death, he gave new life to countless others.

Can you imagine giving your life for someone—intentionally exchanging your life so that someone else can continue to live? Can you imagine giving your life in exchange for someone who doesn't even know you or has spoken badly about you? A member of the armed forces, for example, is trained and thinks nothing of giving their life for the life of someone they do not even know. And such is the mindset of a parent who donates an organ to their child who has a life-threatening illness or injury.

GOING DEEPER

Sheep are animals of prey, meaning that they are much more likely to be hunted than to hunt. Sheep will often freeze instead of fighting. Instead of fending off a predator, sheep will gather into a group for safety in numbers. First Peter 5:8

tells us to "Be sober-minded; be watchful. Your adversary the devil prowls around like a roaring lion, seeking someone to devour." The devil is not going to stop prowling around us. He's not going to become tired, and he's never going to give up. Even when we put on the whole armor of God (Eph 6:10–18), even when we stick together with God as our focus (Eccl 4:12), and even when we utilize prayer as our most powerful weapon (Jas 5:15–16), the devil always returns and always lurks around, hoping to find a way into our lives, even disguising himself as an "angel of light" (2 Cor 11:14).

In the beginning, God created a perfect garden. When sin entered the world, man began to turn toward his own way of thinking, which was contrary to God's way of peace and truth. "The wages of sin is death" (Rom 6:23), and we often go astray and move toward sin when we, like sheep, go our own way and do not heed guidance. Sheep tend to have a strong need for togetherness; thus, a flock will stay together and move together. A single sheep will become agitated immediately when separated from the flock. This is how we stray from the flock of the church: "All we like sheep have gone astray; we have turned—every one—to his own way; and the LORD has laid on him the iniquity of us all." That comparison is in Isaiah 53:6, that we, like sheep, will often follow anything and everything that distracts us from the straight and narrow way that leads to eternal life.

I read once that cattle are driven; sheep are led.[1] Cattle are often prodded from behind and chased by cowboys on horses. Not so with sheep. A shepherd develops a relationship with the flock and leads the sheep where they will find suitable land and calm water and be safe. The flock will follow the shepherd because of the connection, the communication, the protection. The bond between a shepherd and sheep was widely known to biblical authors. David saw this comparison easily,[2] as he compares the Lord to a shepherd who "leads me beside still waters" (Ps 23:2) and "leads me in paths of righteousness for his name's sake" (Ps 23:3).

David continues his poetic metaphor in verse 4: "Even though I walk through the valley of the shadow of death, I will fear no evil, for you are with me; your rod and your staff, they comfort me." A shepherd has a rod and a staff.[3] The rod is used not against the sheep, as some myths would have us believe, but is most often used against predators. The rod is a defensive weapon to keep danger away from the flock. It is also a symbol of authority, seen by sheep as an extension of the shepherd to identify the shepherd as the leader and protector. A skilled shepherd can even wield a rod as a means to guide sheep into a preferred and safer path.

The staff is similar to a rod but is bent into a hook at one end. A staff, also known as a crook, is a tool that not only is described in the Bible, but also remains a traditional herding tool even in modern use. The end that is bent (the hook) can be gently yet firmly used to secure a sheep around the chest to remove it from danger. The hook can also be positioned in such a way to pull a sheep around in order to return it to the herd.

Imagine the strength that is necessary to remove a full-grown sheep from a ditch or mud or another such obstacle. Being rescued is probably uncomfortable at times, and a sheep will likely protest and even resist. The shepherd knows what is best, though, and has the sheep's best interest and restoration in mind.

Likewise, being guided when we stray is not often a comfortable experience. We hear the phrase, "The preacher sure stepped on my toes!" Let's hope that this is a compliment to the messenger and not a complaint! In Luke 15:3–7, Jesus shares a parable with the Pharisees and scribes. He tells them about the importance of seeking out the one sinner who needs someone to find them and bring them back. The shepherd in the story, upon finding his lost sheep, lifts it onto his shoulders and happily carries it back. We don't know if the sheep is injured or not, but it's a personal quest for the shepherd. It's not just *a* sheep that is lost; it's *his* sheep. Look at verse 6: "And when he comes home, he calls together his friends and his neighbors, saying to them, 'Rejoice with me, for I have found *my* sheep that was lost'" (emphasis added). How often are we searching for someone who has strayed? Or are we content with staying in the fold with others "who need no repentance" (Luke 15:7)?

No doubt shepherds rescue sheep time after time. One can only wonder if a shepherd gets tired of counting and searching and redeeming every time a sheep strays from the flock. Does the shepherd finally give up and conclude that the sheep should now find its own way back? We might feel that way with Christians who wander away. Perhaps it's a parent who has relapsed after 100 days of sobriety from a drug addiction. Or it might be a college student who moves away from home and doesn't feel comfortable about finding a local congregation to call home. Or it might even be a visitor who knows nothing about the steadfast love of the Lord. "And let us not grow weary of doing good, for in due season we will reap, if we do not give up" (Gal 6:9). Instead, let us follow the example of the Good Shepherd and repeatedly search out those who need to be led back to the fold.[4]

WRAPPING IT UP

When we spend time in God's word, meditating and asking God to lead us, we will begin to recognize His voice and not stray from following Him. We will not be fooled by the thief who tries to climb in another way because the thief does not know us as the Good Shepherd knows us. May we continue to listen and know the voice of our Good Shepherd and flee from the one whose voice we do not recognize. Our Good Shepherd knows us and knows everything about us. He recognizes us, even when we have fallen and don't even recognize ourselves. We have a Shepherd who will search for us when we stray and who will care for us.

Teddy Copeland wrote a lesson on "Redemption" in the Radiant Study Series *In Christ Alone*. As the lesson concludes, she shares the following inspirational thought: "If I had been the only sinner on earth, God still would have sent His Son for me. It's why in my Bible, in John 3:16, I've crossed out the words 'the world' and filled in my own name. God's love was such that He gave Jesus for me!"[5]

PRAYER

Thank You for being my Shepherd and being willing to face danger in my place. Thank You for knowing me and recognizing me, even when I sometimes don't even recognize myself because of my sinful thoughts and actions. If I will but follow, You will truly lead me beside still waters and in paths of righteousness. I do not have to fear anything, for You are always with me. Create in me a desire to follow Your example and search out those who are lost and gently lead them back to the fold, for Your name's sake.

FOUNDATIONAL QUESTIONS

1. How would people living during the time of the Bible have understood this metaphor in their historical and cultural context(s)?
2. How does God's choice of this metaphor help you better understand the way He views His people?
3. How does this metaphor enhance your understanding of the relationship between Christ and the church? Of your personal relationship with Jesus?
4. What does this metaphor help you learn about your individual role and personal responsibility as part of Christ's church?
5. How can the church as a community better embody this metaphor?
6. How might this metaphor help you explain the church to non-believers?
7. Are there any challenges that arise from misusing, misapplying, or over-emphasizing this metaphor?

GROUP DISCUSSION

1. Despite Jesus being the perfect Shepherd, what are some ways Christians can act like cattle instead of sheep in their relationship with Him?
2. Discuss some ways common spiritual dangers have threatened or harmed your spiritual community.
3. There is strength in numbers. How can we, individually and as a church, protect the flock from danger?
4. The parable of the lost sheep highlights the importance of seeking and caring for those who have

strayed from the flock. How can we model this in our actions and attitudes to ensure that every member feels valued and sought after, especially those who may be drifting away or struggling? How can we create an environment where people feel safe, supported, and encouraged to return to the fold?

5. In what ways can discipline and guidance, symbolized in Psalm 23 as the Lord's rod and staff, be a source of comfort and rescue?

PERSONAL REFLECTION

1. Reflect on a time in your life when you felt lost or directionless. How did you find guidance or support during this time?
2. List specific ways you can more effectively hear the voice of Shepherd and stay connected to the flock. Consider choosing a friend to help you remain accountable if this is a struggle for you.
3. Identify a person, practice, or tool that is a "rod and staff" in your life. How does this bring you comfort and guidance?

Conclusion: Metaphors and Their Limitations

Jeanne Foust and Autumn Richardson

WHEN THE PSALMIST WROTE, "The Lord is my shepherd," he was using a metaphor to think about a way of picturing God—as a caring, nurturing, protective God. David knew the characteristics of both shepherds and sheep personally, and he made a connection between them and his reflections on his own relationship with God! That is exactly what metaphors do: They give us another lens to help us see things differently. We hope *Portraits of God's People* has offered you a fresh perspective about the many ways God sees us as His church: the bride, the family, the body, God's building, the kingdom, a royal priesthood, branches on a vine, the flock. Each portrait provides a unique lens through which we can see not only our spiritual identity but also our special relationship with Him.

You might have noticed that there is some overlap in many of these metaphors. Think of them like tiles of a beautiful mosaic which, although individual pieces, together give us a clearer picture of us as God's people. Despite their separate implications, ultimately they tell a similar story. God's character does not change, but each metaphor may show us a variety of traits in His character. The fact that He values us as His people, for instance, comes through in several of the word pictures He supplies through Scripture. And our roles may not change vastly among the metaphors; we are still subject to Him and dependent on Him for every good thing. These overlaps serve to reinforce the picture He is painting about who we are in Him.

But metaphors do have their limitations. They can be useful to help us see something in a new way, but they are merely ways to compare two seemingly unrelated things. The analogies do not always hold true for *every* characteristic of the comparisons. To use a simple example, if I say my home is my castle, I may mean it provides solace and comfort and privacy and safety. I may even mean I am the "queen" of my home and enjoy some control over what happens there. But I may NOT be saying anything at all about the size or extravagance of my house. And I certainly would not be implying that I have a large staff of people to complete all my household chores for me! The danger comes when we overextend the comparison and read into the metaphor characteristics not implied by the whole of Scripture.

Wayne Grudem writes, "The wide range of metaphors used for the church in the New Testament should remind us not to focus exclusively on any one."[1] Certainly, a single metaphor can be a useful Bible study tool, but the beauty of the range of metaphors used through Scripture is the fuller picture they collectively provide of a God who knows and loves His people and who desires a strong, healthy, and close relationship with them.

Questions to Ask at the End of the Study

1. What are the benefits and limitations of using metaphors to describe the people of God?
2. Which metaphor resonated the most with you in this study? Why do you think this one stands out to you, and how does it shape your understanding and view of the church?
3. What other metaphors for the church do we find in the Bible, and what can we learn from them?
4. Can you think of a new metaphor to illustrate God's people that is not used in Scripture? How could it help others understand the church?

Appendix A—Prayers

CH 1 — The Bride

> Beloved God, form me into the bride You desire me to be. Lead me to grow in purity, faithfulness, and unwavering devotion to You as I await the return of the Bridegroom. Help me to remain spotless and continually cleansed by the precious blood of Jesus.

CH 2 — The Family

> Abba Father, allow me to feel Your presence as my loving Father. You have given me a place where I am welcomed and accepted, and I thank You for Your providential care. Open my eyes to the family I have around me, and show me how to support and love my brothers and sisters in Christ.

CH 3 — The Body

Faithful Creator, thank You for the beautifully diverse body of Christ. Open doors for me to work together with my fellow Christians to be the hands and feet of Jesus as we submit to Him as our head. Remind me that no gift or role is insignificant and that every one of us is needed and essential to the church's mission.

CH 4 — God's Building

Holy God, thank You for Your intimate presence in my life. Fill me with Your holiness, removing all impurities from my life. Thank You for sending Your Son and Your Spirit to show that You will always be with Your people. Strengthen me to contribute to building up Your church and never to be guilty of tearing it down. Live in and through me, oh my Lord and my God.

CH 5 — The Kingdom

Eternal King and Sovereign Lord, reign in me. Help me to live as a faithful citizen of the kingdom of heaven as I strive to do Your will through love, justice, mercy, and peace. Use me to expand Your kingdom through the good news that the Prince of Peace rose from the dead and sits on the throne. May Your will be done on earth as it is in heaven.

CH 6 — A Royal Priesthood

Righteous God, thank You for honoring me with a place in Your royal priesthood. Enable me to come before Your throne without fear, knowing Your love provides a way for us to be reconciled with You. Allow me to see others as You see them and to become a mediator so they may experience Your love, kindness, and forgiveness.

CH 7 — Branches on the Vine

Lord, keep me connected to You always. Help me to draw my strength, sustenance, and nourishment from You so that I may grow and bear fruit. Prune me when there are sins or distractions present in my life. Enable the fruit I bear to glorify and bring honor to Your name.

CH 8 — The Flock

Good Shepherd, thank You for being my Shepherd and being willing to face danger in my place. Thank You for knowing me and recognizing me, even when I sometimes don't even recognize myself because of my sinful thoughts and actions. If I will but follow, You will truly lead me beside still waters and in paths of righteousness. I do not have to fear anything, for You are always with me. Create in me a desire to follow Your example and search out those who are lost and gently lead them back to the fold, for Your name's sake.

Appendix B—Questions

FOUNDATIONAL QUESTIONS

(first set of questions at the end of every chapter)

1. How would people living during the time of the Bible have understood this metaphor in their historical and cultural context(s)?
2. How does God's choice of this metaphor help you better understand the way He views His people?
3. How does this metaphor enhance your understanding of the relationship between Christ and the church? Of your personal relationship with Jesus?
4. What does this metaphor help you learn about your *individual* role and *personal* responsibility as part of Christ's church?

5. How can the church as a *community* better embody this metaphor?
6. How might this metaphor help you explain the church to non-believers?
7. Are there any challenges that arise from misusing, misapplying, or over-emphasizing this metaphor?

Questions to Ask at the End of the Study

1. What are the benefits and limitations of using metaphors to describe the people of God?
2. Which metaphor resonated the most with you in this study? Why do you think this one stands out to you, and how does it shape your understanding and view of the church?
3. What other metaphors for the church do we find in the Bible, and what can we learn from them?
4. Can you think of a new metaphor to illustrate God's people that is not used in Scripture? How could it help others understand the church?

CH 1 — The Bride

GROUP DISCUSSION

1. In the Prophets, we see God's reactions to the unfaithfulness of His people, both His hurt and His forgiveness. What insight does this give us into the relationship of Jesus with His church?
2. What are some ways that Christians, as Christ's bride, might live in adultery?
3. How does understanding baptism as a cleansing and preparation for Christ influence our view of this act? In

what practical ways can the church ensure we are "properly dressed" as a bride waiting for Jesus's return?

4. How can we encourage others to see themselves as the bride of Christ and live accordingly?

5. Thinking about the theme of forgiveness in God's relationship with Israel, how can we mirror this in our church and community?

PERSONAL REFLECTION

1. Think of a time you were unfaithful to Christ. How did you or can you restore that relationship? In what ways did you or can you experience forgiveness and renewed commitment?

2. What specific actions and decisions can help you strengthen your commitment and faithfulness to Christ, similar to the way a wife continually commits to her husband?

3. What are some specific ways you can practice selfless, sacrificial love in your everyday interactions, mirroring Christ's love for the church?

CH 2 – The Family

GROUP DISCUSSION

1. Reflect on families in Scripture that were dysfunctional. Discuss why and how God still used them, even in their "messiness." How can this translate to our imperfect congregations?

2. What are some practices, rituals, and customs that families observe to remain strong and connected that are also important for spiritual families?

3. Why might some people struggle with the concept of church as a family? How can we help them?
4. What can our church do to help integrate new members into our spiritual community so they feel like part of the family and see us as their "soft place to fall"?
5. How can we model being a family as a congregation to our local community?

PERSONAL REFLECTION

1. Thinking about your family of origin, identify any areas where you struggle with the family metaphor and explore ways you can work to overcome those challenges.
2. Think about your roles in your local church. In what ways can you be a more supportive and loving sister?
3. What effect should being a "child of God" have on the way you view yourself? How should it influence the way you interact with others?

CH 3 – The Body

GROUP DISCUSSION

1. What are some of the functions in the church that seem to get the most attention and appreciation? What roles seem to go unnoticed or be less valued?
2. How do feelings of insignificance or being overlooked affect members of the church? What can we do to make sure everyone feels valued and foster a sense of belonging?

3. The hand, ears, and mouth all have very different functions, yet each must perform those functions well to contribute to the overall health, and even existence, of the body. Discuss this concept of unity through diversity as it relates to the body of Christ.

4. How can understanding the interdependence of the body help us resolve conflict and promote unity within the church?

5. How can we each ensure we are actively contributing to the body in a way that aligns with our unique gifts and abilities?

*Consider providing a spiritual gifts assessment for individuals to complete. Follow up with a discussion on how each person can use their gifts to contribute to and improve the health of the body.

PERSONAL REFLECTION

1. Reflect on a time when a "small" part of the church body played a significant role in your life or the life of your congregation. How does this impact your understanding of community and the body of Christ?

2. Identify someone in your congregation who may feel overlooked or undervalued. Write a letter of encouragement to them, acknowledging and thanking them for their contribution or role.

3. Create a personal plan outlining how you can use your gifts and talents to serve the church over the next month or year. Include specific actions, such as visiting widows, painting a classroom, teaching a class, etc.

CH 4 – God's Building

GROUP DISCUSSION

1. Why do you think God chose different types of "buildings" at different times in history? Compare His Old Testament dwellings to His dwelling now. What is the significance of the similarities and differences?

2. In light of how people experienced God's presence through His dwelling places, what does it mean for Him to dwell in us? How should this affect our view of the future?

3. We sing the song, "O Lord, prepare me to be a sanctuary... ." The tabernacle and temple were built by the hands of men, but we are formed by God to be His dwelling. What does that tell you about yourself and the church?

4. How can it be simultaneously true that the church is God's building, but He dwells in heaven, and the church hasn't yet arrived at heaven?

5. How should regarding our bodies as the temple of God affect our behavior and choices? How can we support each other in living this out?

PERSONAL REFLECTION

1. Does your identity as God's dwelling place bring you peace or make you uncomfortable? Why do you think that is?

2. What do you see as your role(s) in making God's building suitable for Him to dwell in?

3. Identify an area of your life that needs to grow in holiness. What guidance can you seek from other Christians? What habits or routines can you incorporate to foster that growth?

CH 5 – The Kingdom

GROUP DISCUSSION

1. What is the relationship between the church as the present expression of the kingdom of God and the kingdom's future consummation? What is it like to live in this tension of "already but not yet"?
2. Discuss struggles you have experienced as citizens of a spiritual kingdom living in a physical one.
3. Matthew 6:19–34 discusses the battle to focus on material things versus spiritual things. What does it look like to seek first the kingdom of God (v. 33) in our personal decisions and priorities?
4. Matthew 25 lists six categories of people that those invited into the kingdom served. How can we seek out each of these populations and minister to them?
5. If proclaiming or heralding is a primary mission of the kingdom, how can we better equip and encourage each other in this responsibility?

PERSONAL REFLECTION

1. How can I align my everyday actions more with the ethics of God's kingdom, such as peace, justice, humility, and righteousness?
2. In what areas of my life do I not always allow God to be King? How can I more fully surrender to His

Lordship?

3. Look at Scriptures that list actions or attitudes that can keep us from inheriting the kingdom of God. Choose one that you actively struggle with and determine how you will better fight against it in the coming weeks.

CH 6 – A Royal Priesthood

GROUP DISCUSSION

1. In what ways can we ensure we do not develop arrogant attitudes in our "elite" position as a royal priesthood of God?
2. What impact does our being holy and "peculiar people" have on our interactions with the world? How is this at tension with our role as priestly mediators between God and people?
3. Thinking of the diverse responsibilities of priesthood, how can we better identify, value, and uplift the roles of everyone in the church, regardless of age or gender?
4. Discuss how an absence of love can undermine our ministry efforts, and identify steps we can take to present a genuine, love-driven approach to service.
5. What are some practical ways we can avoid the pitfalls of the Levite and priest in the parable of the Good Samaritan and willingly wade into the "messiness" of others' lives to bring comfort and healing?

PERSONAL REFLECTION

1. How can confidence to approach God's throne without fear transform the way you pray?
2. How do you handle feelings of inadequacy or unworthiness in light of being part of God's royal priesthood? What are some Scriptures that can help you see yourself as God sees you?
3. Can you think of a time when being part of a "peculiar people" was uncomfortable for you? How did you handle that situation? What are some ways you can stand out in a positive way in your daily interactions?

CH 7 – Branches on the Vine

GROUP DISCUSSION

1. What are some of the spiritual nutrients we rely on to sustain our growth? What happens when we don't access those regularly?
2. What kinds of things hinder growth, cause disease, or cause us to wilt on the vine?
3. Christians go through seasons just like plants— times of dormancy, times of growth, and times of bearing fruit. How can we best support each other in those different seasons?
4. What kinds of fruit should we bear for Christ, individually and collectively?
5. How can we foster a spiritually nourishing environment, much like a greenhouse for plants, so our people can grow and bear fruit?

PERSONAL REFLECTION

1. What habits, practices, or relationships make you feel most connected to the vine? Are there ways that you feel disconnected?
2. Think of a time of pruning in your life. How did this help you grow? Is there anything currently in your life that is hindering growth and needs to be pruned?
3. Think of someone in your spiritual community who seems dormant or disconnected from the vine. How can you help provide that person with spiritual nourishment?

CH 8 – The Flock

GROUP DISCUSSION

1. Despite Jesus being the perfect Shepherd, what are some ways Christians can act like cattle instead of sheep in their relationship with Him?
2. Discuss some common spiritual dangers that have threatened or harmed your spiritual community.
3. There is strength in numbers. How can we, individually and as a church, guard against danger for the protection of the flock?
4. The parable of the lost sheep highlights the importance of seeking and caring for those who have strayed from the flock. How can we model this in our actions and attitudes to ensure that every member feels valued and sought after, especially those who may be drifting away or struggling? How can we create an environment where people feel safe, supported, and encouraged to return to the fold?

5. In what ways can discipline and guidance, symbolized in Psalm 23 as the Lord's rod and staff, be a source of comfort and rescue?

PERSONAL REFLECTION

1. Reflect on a time in your life when you felt lost or directionless. How did you find guidance or support during this time?
2. List specific ways you can more effectively hear the voice of Jesus and stay connected to the flock. Consider choosing a friend to help you remain accountable if this is a struggle for you.
3. Identify a person, practice, or tool that is a "rod and staff" in your life. How does this bring you comfort and guidance?

Appendix C—Scripture Writing Plans

CH 1 – The Bride

Song of Solomon 4:10–11

Song of Solomon 8:6–7

Isaiah 54:5–6

Isaiah 61:10

Isaiah 62:4–5

Jeremiah 2:2

Jeremiah 2:32

Jeremiah 3:1

Jeremiah 31:31–32

Ezekiel 16:8

Ezekiel 16:13–14

Ezekiel 16:15, 22

Ezekiel 16:30–32

Ezekiel 16:58–59

Ezekiel 16:60, 62–63

Hosea 2:19-20

Malachi 2:11

Matthew 9:14–15

Matthew 25:10–12

Mark 2:18–20

Luke 5:33–35

John 3:27–29

John 14:2–3

2 Corinthians 11:2

Ephesians 2:22–24

Ephesians 2:25–27

Ephesians 2:28–32

Revelation 19:7–9

Revelation 21:2–3

Revelation 21:9–11

Revelation 22:17

CH 2 – The Family

Isaiah 65:9

Matthew 23:8–9

Matthew 25:37–40

Mark 3:32–35

John 1:12–13

Acts 3:25

Acts 13:26

Romans 8:14–17

Romans 8:22–23

Romans 8:29

Romans 9:3–4

Romans 9:6–8

1 Corinthians 8:11–13

Galatians 3:26, 29

Galatians 4:4–7

Galatians 4:26–28, 31

Ephesians 1:5

Ephesians 3:14–16

1 Thessalonians 4:9–10

1 Timothy 5:1–2

Hebrews 2:10–13

Hebrews 2:14, 17

Hebrews 12:5–8

Hebrews 12:9–10

1 Peter 1:22–23

1 John 3:1–2

1 John 3:9–10

1 John 3:14–17

1 John 4:20–5:1

1 John 5:2–4

1 John 5:18

CH 3 – The Body

Genesis 1:26–27

Matthew 26:26–27

Mark 14:22–24

Luke 22:19–20

Romans 8:29–30

Romans 12:4–5

1 Corinthians 6:15–17

1 Corinthians 10:16–17

1 Corinthians 11:23–25

1 Corinthians 11:26–29

1 Corinthians 12:12–13

1 Corinthians 12:14–16

1 Corinthians 12:17–21

1 Corinthians 12:22–24

1 Corinthians 12:25–27

1 Corinthians 15:47–49

2 Corinthians 3:18

Ephesians 1:22–23

Ephesians 2:14–16

Ephesians 3:4–6

Ephesians 4:1–4

Ephesians 4:11–13

Ephesians 4:15–16

Ephesians 4:23–25

Ephesians 5:22–24

Ephesians 5:25–27

Ephesians 5:28–30

Colossians 1:15, 18

Colossians 1:24

Colossians 2:18–19

Colossians 3:12–15

CH 4 – God's Building

Exodus 40:34, 38

Leviticus 26:11–12

1 Samuel 2:35

1 Chronicles 17:11–12

2 Chronicles 2:5–6

Psalm 118:21–23

Isaiah 28:16

Isaiah 66:1–2

Ezekiel 37:26–28

Amos 9:11–12

Zechariah 6:12–13

Matthew 21:42–44

Luke 9:33–35

John 2:19–21

John 14:2–3

Acts 4:11–12

Acts 7:46–50

Acts 15:16–18

Acts 17:24–25

1 Corinthians 3:9–11

1 Corinthians 3:16–17

1 Corinthians 6:19–20

2 Corinthians 5:1–3

2 Corinthians 6:16

Ephesians 2:19–22

1 Timothy 3:15

Hebrews 3:3–6

1 Peter 2:4–5

1 Peter 2:6–8

Revelation 3:12

Revelation 21:3

CH 5 – The Kingdom

Isaiah 9:6–7

Daniel 2:44

Daniel 7:27

Matthew 5:3, 10

Matthew 5:19–20

Matthew 7:21

Matthew 13:24–25

Matthew 13:31–32

Matthew 13:33

Matthew 13:44

Matthew 13:45–46

Matthew 13:47–48

Matthew 13:52

Matthew 16:17–19

Matthew 18:1–4

Matthew 25:34–36

Mark 9:1

Luke 1:30–33

Luke 10:8–11

Luke 12:22, 31–32

Luke 17:20–21

John 3:3–5

John 18:36

Romans 14:17

1 Corinthians 6:9–10

1 Corinthians 15:50

Galatians 5:19–21

1 Thessalonians 1:4–5

2 Peter 1:10–11

Hebrews 12:28–29

Revelation 5:9–10

CH 6 – A Royal Priesthood

Exodus 19:4–6

Psalm 101:6

Psalm 132:7–9

Psalm 132:14–16

Isaiah 61:6

Jeremiah 31:14

Zechariah 6:12–13

Acts 26:16–18

Romans 15:15–16

Hebrews 2:17–18

Hebrews 3:1–2

Hebrews 4:14–16

Hebrews 5:4–6

Hebrews 5:7–10

Hebrews 6:18–20

Hebrews 7:1–3

Hebrews 7:11, 14

Hebrews 7:15–17

Hebrews 7:20–22

Hebrews 7:23–25

Hebrews 7:26–28

Hebrews 8:1–2

Hebrews 8:3–4, 6

Hebrews 9:11–12

Hebrews 9:24–26

Hebrews 10:19–22

1 Peter 2:4–5

1 Peter 2:9–10

Revelation 1:5–6

Revelation 5:9–10

Revelation 20:6

CH 7 – Branches on the Vine

Psalm 80:8–11

Psalm 80:14–15

Isaiah 4:2–3

Isaiah 5:1–2

Isaiah 5:3–6

Isaiah 5:7

Isaiah 11:1–2

Isaiah 60:21

Jeremiah 2:21

Jeremiah 5:9–11

Jeremiah 11:16–17

Jeremiah 23:5–6

Jeremiah 33:15–16

Ezekiel 36:8–9

Hosea 14:4–7

Zechariah 6:12

Luke 6:43–45

Luke 8:11–13

Luke 8:14–15

John 15:1–4

John 15:5–8

John 15:16

Romans 11:16–18

Romans 11:19–21

Romans 11:22–24

1 Corinthians 15:20–23

Galatians 5:22–23

Philippians 1:9–11

Colossians 1:9–10

James 1:18

James 3:17–18

CH 8 – The Flock

1 Kings 22:17

Psalm 23:1–2

Psalm 78:52–53

Psalm 78:70–72

Isaiah 40:10–11

Isaiah 53:6–7

Jeremiah 23:3–4

Jeremiah 50:6

Ezekiel 34:8–9

Ezekiel 34:11–12

Ezekiel 34:14–15

Ezekiel 34:20–22

Ezekiel 34:23–24

Micah 2:12

Micah 7:14

Matthew 9:35–36

Matthew 10:5–7

Matthew 18:12–14

Matthew 25:32–33

Matthew 26:31

Luke 15:4–7

John 1:29

John 10:1–35

Acts 20:28–29

Romans 8:35–37

Hebrews 13:20–21

I Peter 1:18–19

I Peter 2:24–25

I Peter 5:2–4

Revelation 7:16–17

Notes

1. The Bride

1. *The Book of Common Prayer*, 1928 ed. (New York: Oxford University Press, 1993), 41.
2. Vermon Pierre, *Dearly Beloved: How God's Love for the Church Deepens Our Love For Each Other* (Chicago: Moody, 2024), 169.
3. Pierre, *Dearly Beloved*, 176.
4. Pierre, *Dearly Beloved*, 175.
5. Steven Markantonis, "The Spousal Mystery: A Historical Survey of the Relationship of the Bridegroom and Bride," *The Dunwoodie Review* 35 (2012): 112.
6. Markantonis, "The Spousal Mystery," 115.
7. Markantonis, "The Spousal Mystery," 117.
8. Markantonis, "The Spousal Mystery," 118.
9. Garland Elkins and Thomas B. Warren, eds., *The Church—The Beautiful Bride of Christ* (Jonesboro, AR: National Christian Press, 1980), 180.
10. Carolyn Osiek, "The Bride of Christ (Ephesians 5:22–33): A Problematic Wedding," *Biblical Theology Bulletin* 32:1 (2022): 34.
11. E. M. Zerr, *1 Corinthians–Revelation*, vol. 6 of Zerr's Bible Commentary (Athens, AL: Truth Publications, 2018), 112.
12. Merriam-Webster Dictionary Online, "Pure," 2024.
13. Jay Lockhart and David L. Roper, *Truth for Today Commentary: Ephesians and Philippians*, ed. Eddie Cloer (Searcy, AR: Resource Publications, 2009), 284.
14. Jim McGuiggan, *The Book of Revelation* (Lubbock, TX: Sunset Institute Press, 2011), 325.
15. James Burton Coffman, *Commentary on Galatians, Ephesians, Philippians, and Colossians* (Austin, TX: Firm Foundation, 1977), 224.
16. Charles Van Zyl and Lilly Nortjé-Meyer, "The Metaphor of 'Walking in Love' as Matrix for the Familial Relationships in Ephesians 5:22–6:9," *Pharos Journal of Theology* 99 (2018): 7.
17. Albert Barnes, *Barnes' Notes on the New Testament: Eph.–Col.* (Grand Rapids: Baker, 1963), 110.
18. Lockhart and Roper, *Ephesians and Philippians*, 295.
19. Kerry Knight, "Relation of Husbands and Wives Explained by the Relation of Christ and the Church (5:22–32)" in *The Book of Ephesians*, ed. Garland Elkins and Thomas B. Warren (Memphis: Sain Publications, 1984), 203.
20. Barnes, *Eph.–Col.*, 110.
21. Lockhart and Roper, *Ephesians and Philippians*, 283.

22. Lockhart and Roper, *Ephesians and Philippians*, 283.
23. Lockhart and Roper, *Ephesians and Philippians*, 284.
24. Sandra Madden, "Ephesians 5:22–33: Rethinking Submission," *Lutheran Forum* 53:2 (2019): 22.

2. The Family

1. Lanny Wolfe, *God's Family*, Cleveland, TN: Pathway Music, 1974.

3. The Body

1. Michael Peppard, "Powerful Sons Were Adopted Sons: A Roman Imperial Perspective," *The Bible and Interpretation*, Dec 2012, https://bibleinterp.arizona.edu/articles/pep368014.
2. Menander, *Mendandri Dycolus*, Oxford Classical Texts (Oxford: Oxford University Press, 1960), 729–39.

4. God's Building

1. Francis Brown, S. R. Driver, and Charles A. Briggs, "בית," in *A Hebrew and English Lexicon of the Old Testament* (Peabody, MA: Hendrickson, 2012), 108–110.

5. The Kingdom

1. Edmon Gallagher, *The Sermon on the Mount* (Florence, AL: Heritage Christian University Press, 2021), 23.
2. Gallagher, *The Sermon on the Mount*, 22–23.

6. A Royal Priesthood

1. Merriam-Webster Dictionary Online, "Royal," 2024.
2. Merriam-Webster Dictionary Online, "Priest," 2024.
3. Peter H. Hobbie, "I Peter 2:2–10," *Interpretation* 47.2 (1993): 170–73.
4. I originally got this from a sermon by my eldest son, Rob Sparks, who had gotten it from a book. I could not find the book, so I cannot source it beyond Rob.
5. Claire Ansberry, "The Mental-Health Benefits of Going to Church," *WSJ*, 13 April 2024.
6. James Freeman, "Are Faith and Family Staging a Comeback?," *WSJ*, 19 April 2024.

7. Branches on the Vine

1. Information in this paragraph and the next is taken from 101.school, "Understanding the Growth and Changes in Vine Branches," https://101.school/courses/interaction-of-vine-and-branches-in-producing-grapes/modules/3-life-cycle-of-a-vine/units/3-how-branches-grow-and-change.

8. The Flock

1. Sarah Howley, "Driving Cattle or Leading Sheep Psalm 23," *Inspirit Encourage*, 18 Dec 2018, https://www.inspiritencourage.com/mini/driving-cattle-or-leading-sheep#:~:text=Cattle%20are%20driven%20from%20behind,drive%20that%20moves%20the%20cows.

2. Shereen Lynn, "The Shepherd's Oil," *Equip Her*, 23 June 2011, https://equipherlife.com/2011/06/23/the-shepherds-oil/.

3. Information about the rod and staff is taken from Aaron L. Garriott, "Your Rod and Your Staff, They Comfort Me," *Tabletalk* (Aug 2018): 21–22, https://tabletalkmagazine.com/article/2018/08/your-rod-and-your-staff-they-comfort-me/#:~:text=The%20rod%20and%20staff%20can,provided%20comfort%20to%20the%20sheep.

4. Amanda Idleman, "The Marvelous Meaning of 'Feed My Sheep' in John 21," Crosswalk.com, 31 Jan 2024, https://www.crosswalk.com/faith/bible-study/the-marvelous-meaning-of-feed-my-sheep-in-john-21.html.

5. Teddy Copeland, "Redemption: Ephesians 1:7," in *In Christ Alone: A Look at Blessings in Ephesians 1*, ed. Autumn Richardson and Melissa McFerrin (Florence, AL: Cypress Publications, 2023), 57.

Conclusion: Metaphors and Their Limitations

1. Wayne Grudem, *Systematic Theology: An Introduction to Biblical Doctrine* (Grand Rapids: Zondervan, 1994), 859.

Acknowledgments

I think most people wait and write acknowledgments at the very end of the book creation process. I'm not like most people. I'm actually experiencing a little bit (ok, a LOT) of writer's block and am panicking about the book getting to the printers on time. I can't think of a better time to sit, take a breath, and be grateful for the village that makes projects like this one happen.

This is the second book in the Radiant Study Series, so it is only now officially a series! That is why the first "thank you" goes to you—the reader. So many of you took a chance on us, bought *In Christ Alone* for yourself or your ladies' Bible class, and have been so encouraging in your feedback. We hope this book will bless you as well.

Melissa McFerrin and I co-edit this series. What that really means is that I have wild, ambitious goals for a book. I know who I want on the team to help create the vision, and I get them on board. Melissa, however, possesses the work ethic to get us to the finish line. She spends hours proofreading, reformatting, and nudging me toward my responsibilities while she quietly fulfills hers. This book simply wouldn't be in your hands without her. She possesses wisdom and skill beyond her years, and I'm so thankful to be able to do kingdom work with one of my dearest friends.

To the contributors, whether you wrote a chapter or questions or prayers, please know that you weren't chosen simply because you were willing. You were invited to this project because I see how you live for the Lord and His church, and I knew you could articulate the message I wanted this book to convey. Several of you came into the project late in the game, so I especially thank you for helping out on such short notice.

Thank you to the staff of Heritage Christian University Press for encouraging this project and for their dedication to providing quality resources for churches. The church is more well-equipped because of them. Thanks to Brad McKinnon for granting me way too much time to experiment with styles, fonts, and features on our editing software when he really needed to be working on his dissertation. I'm not an easy person to please when I have a vision in my head, and he bent over backward to help us create a product I could feel proud of. Jamie Cox spent hours handling all the particulars and fine-tuning the product to the printer's specifications. This book just magically appeared in the mail one day thanks to her!

It feels cliché, but I absolutely must thank my family. They have not complained a single time when I've disappeared to the library, my office, or my local meat-and-three for hours to work on this book. They have been patient and gracious when I've talked excitedly about the project or needed to run ideas by them. They know I've found my passion and have been unwavering in cheering me on.

To my God, all the glory belongs to You. There was a time in my life when I wanted the praise and attention for a project like this. Now I understand that's why those projects never actually came to be back then. I lay this all at Your feet to do with what You see fit. I only pray it strengthens Your kingdom.

Autumn Richardson

Contributors

Editors

Melissa McFerrin, M.Min., is the Executive Assistant to the President and Coordinator of Women's Continuing Education at Heritage Christian University. She loves to read, travel, and spend time with her husband, Clay, and their Christian family at the Chisholm Hills Church of Christ.

Autumn Richardson, M.Min., is the Director of Distance Learning, an Instructor of Ministry, and Assistant Coordinator of Women's Continuing Education at Heritage Christian University. She and her husband, Adam, worship with the Petersville Church of Christ in Florence, AL, and have three adult children, a daughter-in-love, and a granddaughter.

Contributors

Lori Boyd, M.A., is a registered nurse and teacher. She has authored several Bible study books for women and speaks regularly at ladies' events. Lori and her husband, Sam, live in Murfreesboro, TN, with their three children and are members of the East Main Church of Christ.

Molly Daily, M.Ed., is the Spanish teacher at the Florence Freshman Center in Florence, AL. She has taught Spanish in public schools throughout the country. She and her husband, Nathan, worship with the Mars Hill Church of Christ, where Nathan is the education minister. They have two children, Scott and Ella, and two dogs, Chewbacca (Chewie) and Willow.

J.J. Davenport, M.A., is the Dean of Arts at Mars Hill Bible School. She has taught music there for 18 years. She is a graduate of Heritage Christian University and holds an M.A. in education. She and her husband, Larry, have two girls, two grandchildren, and two bonus children. They attend the Jackson Heights Church of Christ, where Larry serves as the Young Families minister.

Jeanne Foust, M.A., serves as Instructor of English at Heritage Christian University and is a member of the Radiant ministry team. She and her husband, Kevin, work and worship with the Cross Point Church of Christ in Florence, AL. She enjoys evening boat rides, anything chocolate, most spectator sports, and spending time with her two daughters and her son-in-law.

Tonya Hayes works part-time at Heritage Christian University as an office assistant in Distance Learning. Tonya and her husband, David, worship at Petersville Church of Christ with their three daughters. Tonya is a board member of the Kennedy Douglass Art Center Volunteers. Tonya loves traveling and reading and is always up for a cup of coffee or a craft project.

Ava Johnson is married to Dustin and mom to twin boys, August and Arlo. She enjoys serving the Lord through the Radiant program, Maywood Christian Camp, women's and children's ministries at her home congregation, and her work at Heritage Christian University. Her favorite pastimes are spending time with her family, looking at her family, and telling other people about her family.

Cayron Mann is a Licensed Professional Counselor and one of the partners at Three Cord Counseling, LLC. She worships at the Highland Park congregation in Muscle Shoals, AL. Her son Cameron graduated from Freed Hardeman University in 2024. She also shares her home with three cats: Leia, Ben, and Cosette.

Carol Sparks, M.B.A., is enrolled in the Master of Ministry program at Heritage Christian University. She is blessed with four grown sons and seven grandchildren, lives in Crossville, TN, and worships with the Crossville Church of Christ. Carol enjoys making and mailing cards of encouragement and weaving blankets, shawls, scarves, and towels to give as gifts.

Credits

RADIANT

God's warmth in our hearts. His light in our lives.

our
MISSION

Radiant exists for the purpose of cultivating spiritual formation within the hearts of women. We equip women by providing theologically rich resources and opportunities to serve and study scripture.

our
VISION

Radiant women look to Him in all areas of life and are transformed into the image of Christ.

We offer

CLASSES ONLINE AND ON CAMPUS
WORKSHOPS AND FORUMS
BOOKS, STUDY RESOURCES, AND CONTENT

Learn more at
www.hcu.edu/radiant
or scan the QR code.

Contact Us
Email: radiant@hcu.edu
Phone: (256) 766-6610

Also by Cypress Publications

Radiant Study Series

Portraits of God's People (2024)

In Christ Alone: A Look at Blessings in Ephesians 1 (2023)

Stand-alone Title

Hamblen, Betty. *Women in the Shadows* (2022)

Berean Study Series

The Bond of Peace: The Seven Ones from Ephesians 4 (available 2026)

God Battling for the Heart of His People (available 2025)

Encountering the Gospel (2024)

Led by God's Spirit: A Practical Study of Galatians 5:22–26 (2023)

Majesty and Mercy: God Through the Eyes of Isaiah (2022)

For the Glory of God: Christ and the Church in Ephesians (2021)

Cloud of Witnesses: Ancient Stories of Faith (2020)

Visions of Grace (2019)

Instructions for Living: The Ten Commandments (2018)

Clothed in Christ: A How-to Guide (2017)

What Does Real Christianity Look Like? A Study of the Parables (2016)

The Ekklesia of Christ: Becoming the People of God (2015)

Onesimus Bible Study Series

Joy and Comfort: Favorite Psalms (available 2026)

CYPRESS

To see full catalog of Heritage Christian University Press and
its imprint Cypress Publications, visit
www.hcu.edu/publications